RETIREMENT ISSUES, PLANS AND LIFESTYLES

401(K) PLANS

A SPONSOR'S ROLE IN DEFAULT INVESTMENTS AND AN EXAMINATION OF TARGET DATE FUNDS

RETIREMENT ISSUES, PLANS AND LIFESTYLES

RETIREMENT ISSUES, PLANS AND LIFESTYLES

401(K) PLANS

A SPONSOR'S ROLE IN DEFAULT INVESTMENTS AND AN EXAMINATION OF TARGET DATE FUNDS

WESLEY MEYER
EDITOR

nova publishers
New York

Library of Congress Cataloging-in-Publication Data

ISBN: 978-1-63484-727-8

Published by Nova Science Publishers, Inc. † New York

CONTENTS

PREFACE

Employers who sponsor 401(k) plans report using a range of default investment types to automatically enroll employees in their plans based on each type's design and other attributes. Department of Labor (DOL) created a regulatory "safe harbor" in 2007 to limit plan sponsor liability for investing contributions on behalf of employees into default investments when employees do not otherwise make an election. In addition, DOL identified three default investments that, if selected by sponsors, would qualify a plan for safe harbor protection. This book examines which options plan sponsors selected as default investments and why; how plan sponsors monitor their default investment selections; and what challenges, if any, plan sponsors report facing when adopting a default investment for their plan. Furthermore, this book determines what is known about the effect of automatic enrollment policies among the nation's 401(k) plans, and the extent of and future prospect for such policies; and the potential benefits and limitations of automatic IRA proposals and state-assisted retirement savings proposals.

In: 401(k) Plans
Editor: Wesley Meyer
ISBN: 978-1-63484-727-8

Chapter 1

401(K) PLANS: CLEARER REGULATIONS COULD HELP PLAN SPONSORS CHOOSE INVESTMENTS FOR PARTICIPANTS*

United States Government Accountability Office

WHY GAO DID THIS STUDY

The Department of Labor (DOL) created a regulatory "safe harbor" in 2007 to limit plan sponsor liability for investing contributions on behalf of employees into default investments when employees do not otherwise make an election. In addition, DOL identified three default investments that, if selected by sponsors, would qualify a plan for safe harbor protection. GAO was asked to review certain aspects of these default investment types.

This report examines: (1) which options plan sponsors selected as default investments and why; (2) how plan sponsors monitor their default investment selections; and (3) what challenges, if any, plan sponsors report facing when adopting a default investment for their plan. To answer these questions, GAO reviewed relevant federal laws and guidance; analyzed industry survey data on the prevalence of default investment use; analyzed nongeneralizable responses from 227 plan sponsors who voluntarily completed a GAO web-based questionnaire; and interviewed 96 stakeholders, including service providers,

* This is an edited, reformatted and augmented version of the United States Government Accountability Office publication, GAO-15-578, dated August 2015.

advocacy groups, and research organization representatives, as well as academicians.

What GAO Recommends

GAO recommends that DOL assess the challenges that plan sponsors and stakeholders reported, including the extent to which these challenges can be addressed, and implement corrective actions, as appropriate. DOL generally agreed with GAO's recommendation.

What GAO Found

Employers who sponsor 401(k) plans report using a range of default investment types to automatically enroll employees in their plans based on each type's design and other attributes. From 2009 through 2013, the majority of employers who sponsored 401(k) plans reported using a target-date fund as their default, according to data from three annual industry surveys that GAO reviewed. A target-date fund is a product or portfolio that changes asset allocations and associated risk levels over time with the objective of decreasing risk of losses with increasing age. Fewer plan sponsors reported using the other two default investment types that the Department of Labor (DOL) identified: balanced funds—products with a fixed ratio of equity to fixed-income investments—or managed account services—investment services that use participant information to customize asset allocations. Plan sponsors completing GAO's questionnaire said that they generally looked for asset diversification, ease of participant understanding, limited fiduciary liability, and a fit with participant characteristics when selecting a default investment. Some stakeholders that GAO interviewed also identified positive attributes of each default investment type and highlighted other factors that could influence a plan sponsor's default investment selection, such as plan sponsor preferences; plan circumstances; or changes in the plan's environment like a plan merger or court decision.

Plan sponsors generally monitor plan investments, including default investments, periodically to ensure alignment with the plan's objectives and investment strategies, according to stakeholders GAO interviewed and plan sponsors responding to GAO's questionnaire. Stakeholders that GAO interviewed generally said that the type of default investment and a plan's circumstances— such as the availability of resources and expertise devoted to investment monitoring—can affect the extent of a plan sponsor's monitoring efforts and the response to monitoring results. Plan sponsors responding to GAO's questionnaire and stakeholders GAO interviewed said that after an extensive default selection process, some plan sponsors may be reluctant to change the default investment regardless of monitoring results. For example, a plan sponsor and service provider may have negotiated a reduction in overall plan investment management fees in exchange for using a provider's investment as a plan's default, making it more difficult to change.

Plan sponsors cited regulatory uncertainty, liability protection, and the adoption of innovative products as significant challenges when adopting one of the three default investments. DOL regulations outline several specific conditions that plan sponsors must adhere to in order to receive relief from liability for any investment losses to participants that occur as a result of the investment. Plan sponsors responding to GAO's questionnaire and stakeholders GAO interviewed generally said that the regulations were unclear as to: (1) how sponsors could fulfill the regulatory requirement to factor the ages of participants into their default investment selection; (2) whether each default investment provided the same level of protection; or (3) whether they were allowed to incorporate other retirement features, such as products offering guaranteed retirement income, into a plan's default investment. Such uncertainty could lead some plan sponsors to make suboptimal choices when selecting a plan's default investment that could have long-lasting negative effects on participants' retirement savings.

Abbreviations

DB	defined benefit
DC	defined contribution
DOL	U.S. Department of Labor
EBSA	Employee Benefits Security Administration
ERISA	Employee Retirement Income Security Act of 1974
Form 5500	Form 5500 Annual Return/Report of Employee Benefit Plan
IRA	individual retirement account
PPA	Pension Protection Act of 2006

QDIA	Qualified Default Investment Alternative
TDF	target-date fund

* * *

August 25, 2015

The Honorable Elizabeth Warren
United States Senate

Dear Senator Warren:

While 60 percent of the U.S. private-sector workforce has access to an employer-sponsored defined contribution (DC) retirement plan,[1] many of these workers choose not to participate—potentially increasing their risk in retirement. According to data from the Bureau of Labor Statistics, in 2014, 18 percent of the full-time, private-sector workforce had access to but did not participate in their employer's DC plan.[2] While employers can choose to automatically enroll nonparticipating workers into their plans, as we previously reported, some of them did not, citing fears of liability.[3] To address sponsors' concerns and to bolster participant retirement savings, the Pension Protection Act of 2006 (PPA) included provisions to facilitate plan sponsors' adoption of automatic enrollment programs—policies that allow employers to automatically enroll eligible workers in a company- sponsored plan.[4] Under those provisions, plan sponsors can automatically enroll eligible workers in an employment-based plan's default investment unless such workers explicitly opt out of participation or choose another plan investment option. Because an automatic enrollment program requires plan sponsors—absent a specific choice by the plan participant—to choose an investment vehicle in which to invest contributions, the provisions also provided for the Department of Labor (DOL) to promulgate regulations on the appropriateness of designating default investments that include a mix of asset classes consistent with capital preservation, long-term capital appreciation, or a blend of both.

In 2007, DOL issued final regulations outlining conditions under which a plan fiduciary would generally not be liable for any investment losses that occur as a result of investing contributions on behalf of participants and beneficiaries.[5] To qualify for this fiduciary relief or "safe harbor" protection,[6] among other things, plan sponsors must select one of the following three qualified default investment alternatives (QDIA) as a plan's long-term default investment:[7]

- a product with a mix of investments[8] that takes into account the individual's age or anticipated retirement date, such as a target date fund;
- a product with a mix of investments that takes into account the characteristics of the group of employees as a whole, rather than each individual, such as a balanced fund; or
- an investment service that allocates contributions among existing plan options to provide an asset mix that takes into account the individual's age or retirement date, such as a managed account.

While many plans have adopted automatic enrollment policies and QDIAs in recent years, questions have arisen regarding whether the QDIA types that sponsors select are serving the best interests of all participants or improving the prospects of a secure retirement for participants whose contributions and earnings remain in the QDIA for a lengthy period of time. Thus, you asked us to review certain aspects of the QDIAs that DOL identified.[9] Specifically, we examined:

1. Which options plan sponsors selected as QDIAs and why;
2. How plan sponsors monitor their plans' QDIAs; and
3. What challenges, if any, plan sponsors report facing with regard to the selection and use of QDIAs.

To answer these questions, we reviewed relevant federal laws, regulations, and guidance on the selection and use of QDIAs in 401(k) plans; reviewed relevant research and literature; and interviewed 96 stakeholders, including plan sponsors, service providers, participant advocates, plan sponsor advocates, and academic and other pension experts. We identified knowledgeable stakeholders and selected for interviews those who would provide us with a broad range of perspectives on issues surrounding the use of default investments in DC plans. We analyzed the content of the interview responses and identified common themes. To gather data on the prevalence of QDIA use, we used data from three industry surveys that reported consistent annual data on default investments for the most consecutive years, from 2009 through 2013.[10] We took several steps to assess the reliability of the data from the three surveys, including reviewing related documentation, interviewing knowledgeable officials, and corroborating these findings with relevant literature and interview responses. We found the data to be sufficiently reliable when aggregated, as we do in this report. To better understand the experiences of plan sponsors with respect to QDIA adoption and monitoring efforts, we developed a web-based questionnaire, which was publicized with the assistance of several professional organizations whose memberships included plan sponsors or others who act as plan fiduciaries. We received 227 completed questionnaires from plan sponsors, representing the full range of plan sizes and QDIA types. We analyzed these responses and followed up with 55 respondents who voluntarily provided their contact information—we subsequently interviewed or collected written responses from 28 of these respondents to gain additional insight into their decision to adopt a QDIA for their plan. The responses we received from the questionnaire and follow-up interviews represent the views and experiences of the individual plan sponsors who contacted GAO and cannot be generalized to represent the views of the broader universe of plan sponsors. For more information on the development of the methodology used in this report, see appendix I.

We conducted this performance audit from June 2014 through July 2015 in accordance with generally accepted government auditing standards. Those standards require that we plan and perform the audit to obtain sufficient, appropriate evidence to provide a reasonable basis for our findings and conclusions based on our audit objectives. We believe that the evidence obtained provides a reasonable basis for our findings and conclusions based on our audit objectives.

BACKGROUND

As we previously reported, plan sponsors who automatically enroll employees in 401(k) plans can substantially increase participation rates among their covered employees.[11] Plan sponsors who adopt automatic enrollment policies must select a default investment—a fund or other investment vehicle into which an employee's contributions are invested— unless the employee specifies one or more investments from those available under the plan. As shown in figure 1, the number of plans that reported having automatic enrollment and a default investment has increased significantly since 2009, with more than three times the number of small plans using automatic enrollment and a default investment in 2013.

The adoption of automatic enrollment programs is voluntary. Plan sponsors who adopt automatic enrollment must also establish default contribution rates for workers who do not specify these choices on their own. At their discretion, plan sponsors may choose to automatically enroll all employees, new or recently hired employees, or existing employees into a plan's default investment, which may be a QDIA.[12] Automatic enrollment may occur once—such as when a plan sponsor establishes a new plan or when a merger requires participants in one firm's plan to join the other firm's plan—or on a recurring basis, such as when a plan sponsor elects to re-enroll all participants, including those who have previously made investment elections. Plan sponsors may automatically re-enroll participants for a number of reasons; for example, to improve the diversification of participants' accounts, to adjust to a change in record keeper,[13] or to address the removal of certain investments from a plan's investment lineup. In all circumstances, the sponsor must notify the participants in writing of their right to opt out or to make their own investment elections.[14]

While the choice to offer a QDIA is voluntary, sponsors who choose to offer a QDIA must comply with applicable DOL regulations covering the selection of an appropriate QDIA option to use in order to receive certain fiduciary relief should participants experience investment losses. Some plan sponsors forgo the safe harbor protections and select a non-QDIA default investment, such as a money market fund or a stable value fund. There are a variety of reasons why plan sponsors do this. For example, a sponsor may have few employees and choose to require participants to make an investment election. Another sponsor may not want to assume the burden of implementing and monitoring a QDIA, including sending out multiple notices to participants. Plan sponsors who select a QDIA must adhere to several specific regulatory conditions to receive relief from liability for any investment losses to participants that occur as a result of the investment in a QDIA. To obtain relief, among other things, plan sponsors must provide participants with advance notice of the circumstances under which plan contributions or other assets will be invested on their behalf in a QDIA; a description of the QDIA's investment objectives, risk and return characteristics, and fees and expenses; and the right of participants to opt out of the QDIA.[15]

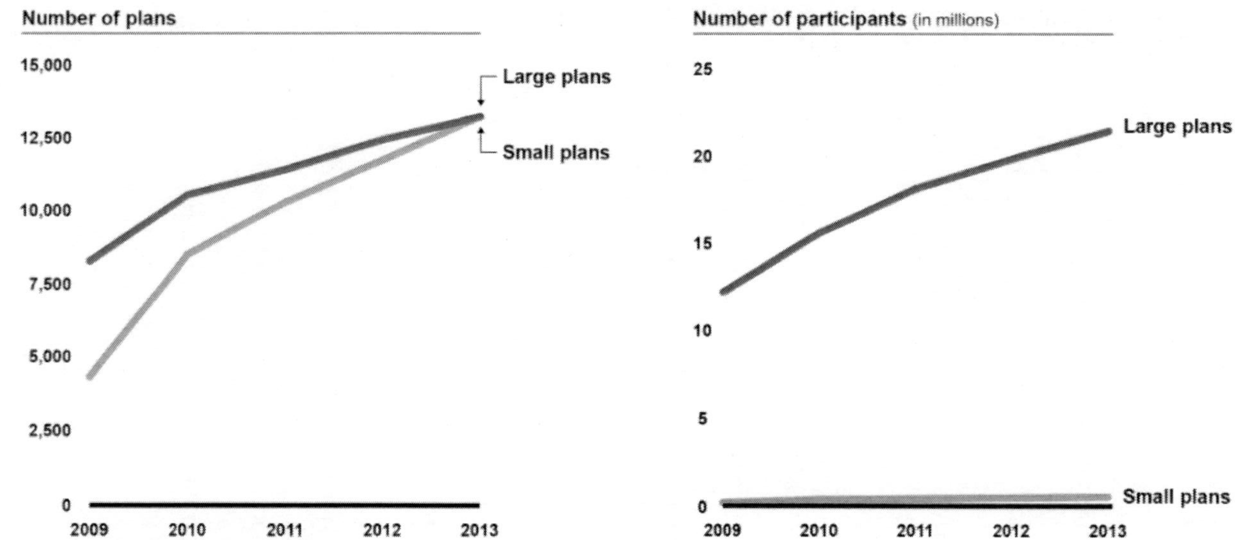

Source: GAO analysis of annual Form 5500 data | GAO-15-578

Note: Participant totals represent the total number of active participants in DC plans with both automatic enrollment and a default investment. DOL's Form 5500 Annual Return/Report of Employee Benefit Plan (Form 5500) is completed by plan sponsors and serves as the primary source of information for both the federal government and the private sector regarding the funding, assets, investments, and fees of pension and other employee benefit plans. The Form 5500 does not require sponsors to report the number of automatically enrolled participants.

Figure 1. Automatic Enrollment and Default Investment Use among Private-Sector Defined Contribution Plans, by Plan Size and Participant Count (2009-2013).

The QDIA regulations were expected to increase average retirement savings and pension retirement incomes for participants and beneficiaries by directing default investments to higher performing portfolios and by promoting the implementation of automatic enrollment programs in participant-directed individual accounts. DOL regulations describe three investment types that qualify as a QDIA that plan sponsors may choose to consider:

1. An investment product or model portfolio that applies generally accepted investment theories; is diversified so as to minimize the risk of large losses; and designed to provide varying degrees of long-term appreciation and capital preservation through a mix of equity and fixed-income exposures based on the participant's age, target retirement date (such as normal retirement age under the plan), or life expectancy. Such products and portfolios change their asset allocations and associated risk levels over time with the objective of becoming more conservative (i.e., decreasing risk of losses) with increasing age. DOL noted that an example of such a fund or portfolio may be a "life-cycle" or "targeted-retirement-date" fund or account.[16] This investment type is hereafter referred to as "target-date funds" (TDF) and can take two forms:[17]
   - **"Off-the-shelf" TDFs:** Pre-packaged retail products that typically use proprietary funds as their component investment options. These funds often have little overlap between the TDF's underlying funds and those in the plan's core investment lineup. Plan sponsors selecting these products have minimal control over the quality or fee levels of the component funds.
   - **Custom TDFs:** Customized products for which a plan sponsor is responsible for selecting the asset classes to include, the funds to use, and the glide path that governs how those asset classes and funds will be allocated over time. Plan sponsors are able to monitor and adjust these custom TDF elements as they do for the plan's other investment options. These products can offer greater diversification than off-the-shelf TDFs because plan sponsors have access to a broader array of investment managers and the ability to incorporate the plan's existing core funds into the investment product.
2. An investment product or model portfolio that applies generally accepted investment theories, is diversified so as to minimize the risk

of large losses, and designed to provide long-term appreciation and capital preservation through a mix of equity and fixed-income exposures consistent with a target level of risk appropriate for participants of the plan as a whole.[18] DOL noted that an example of such a fund or portfolio may be a "balanced" fund, and this investment type is hereafter referred to as "balanced funds."[19]

3. An investment management service with respect to which a plan fiduciary, applying generally accepted investment theories, allocates the assets of a participant's individual account to achieve varying degrees of long-term appreciation and capital preservation through a mix of equity and fixed-income exposures, offered through investment alternatives available under the plan, and based on the participant's age, target retirement date (such as normal retirement age under the plan) or life expectancy. Such portfolios are diversified so as to minimize the risk of large losses and change their asset allocations and associated risk levels for an individual account over time with the objective of becoming more conservative (i.e., decreasing risk of losses) with increasing age. DOL noted that an example of such a service may be a "managed account" and this investment type is hereafter referred to as "managed accounts."[20]

Rather than prescribing the specific actions that a sponsor must take when selecting and monitoring plan investment options the Employee Retirement Income Security Act of 1974 (ERISA) requires that all plan fiduciaries, including plan sponsors,[21] discharge their plan duties solely in the interest of plan participants, with the care, skill, prudence, and diligence that a prudent person acting in a like capacity and familiar with such matters would use.[22] To comply with this requirement when selecting plan investments, including a QDIA, a plan sponsor "must engage in an objective, thorough, and analytical process that involves consideration of the quality of competing providers and investment products, as appropriate."[23] Plan fiduciaries that breach any of their fiduciary duties can be held personally liable to repay any losses, and restore any profits that have been made through use of the assets. They may also face other sanctions—including their removal as a plan fiduciary. Nothing in the QDIA safe harbor relieves any plan fiduciary from the duty to prudently select and monitor any default investments under the plan.[24] According to DOL officials, the monitoring process should examine whether there have been any significant changes in the information fiduciaries considered when the QDIA was first selected or last reviewed. Plan sponsors are typically plan fiduciaries.

In certain circumstances, other entities may also assume a fiduciary role. As we previously reported, managed account providers and record keepers may be fiduciaries, depending on their roles and the services they provide.[25] As with other investment alternatives made available under the plan, fiduciaries must carefully consider investment fees and expenses when choosing a QDIA.

DOL's Employee Benefits Security Administration (EBSA) is the primary agency tasked with enforcing Title I of ERISA, including the PPA provisions, to protect plan participants and beneficiaries from the misuse or theft of their pension assets.[26] To carry out its responsibilities, EBSA issues regulations and guidance; investigates plan sponsors, fiduciaries, and service providers; seeks appropriate remedies to correct violations of the law; and pursues litigation when it deems necessary. As part of its mission, DOL is also responsible for assisting and educating plan sponsors to help ensure the retirement security of workers and their beneficiaries.

Several Factors Led a Majority of Plan Sponsors to Use Target-Date Funds over Other Default Investments

Plan Sponsors Use All Default Investment Types, but Most Use Target-Date Funds

Although there are no nationally representative data on the universe of 401(k) plan sponsors' default investment use,[27] data from three industry surveys indicated that, while plan sponsors used a range of default investment types from 2009 through 2013, the majority of plan sponsors surveyed used a TDF for this purpose.[28] Smaller groups of sponsors surveyed selected balanced funds or managed accounts as a default investment. In fact, in most years a greater percentage of plan sponsors surveyed reported using non-QDIA products—such as stable value funds or money market funds—as their default investments than used balanced funds and managed accounts combined. (See figure 2)

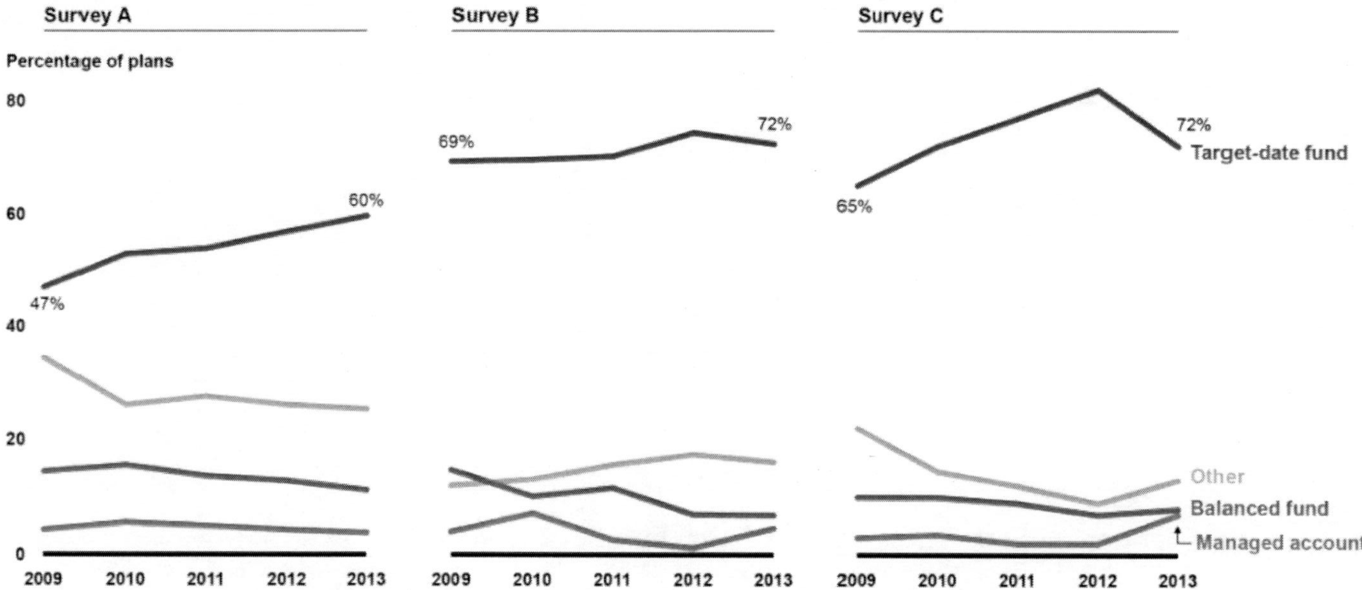

Source: GAO analysis of three industry surveys of sponsors of defined contribution plans. | GAO-15-578

Note: Given that our focus was the prevalence of the use of QDIAs among plan sponsors, we combined all other categories of non-QDIA default investment vehicles that plan sponsors listed in the surveys, reflected as "other" in this figure.

Figure 2. Use of Default Investments in Defined Contribution Plans with Automatic Enrollment, by Investment Type (2009-2013).

Some Sponsors Consider Design Features, Fiduciary Protections, and Participant Characteristics When Selecting a Default Investment

Several stakeholders[29] that we interviewed generally said that plan sponsors looked for design simplicity, fiduciary protection, and a fit with participant characteristics when selecting a default investment. Given that QDIA adoption is voluntary and sponsors have broad discretion in choosing a QDIA, plan sponsors with similar plans may select different QDIA types for the same reason. For example, 2 of the 28 sponsor respondents to our questionnaire that we subsequently interviewed told us that they chose their QDIA type because, in their view, the QDIA they chose best fit the age distribution of their participant population. In one case, the sponsor stated that the age demographics of the plan's employees were diverse, ranging from 21 to 71. As a result, the sponsor chose a TDF, believing that the funds' many target dates best fit the wide spectrum of participant ages within the plan. In contrast, another sponsor noted that the plan's participants had uneven age distribution, with higher percentages of older and younger participants. This sponsor chose a managed account, reasoning that a balanced fund or TDF would have been inappropriate for all employees. Of the 222 plan sponsors who responded to our questionnaire and selected a default investment that was a QDIA, 156 listed asset diversification, 141 listed the ease of understanding by participants, 132 listed limiting fiduciary liability, and 86 listed the appropriateness of a QDIA for a plan's participant demographics among the top reasons for selecting a QDIA.[30] Stakeholders identified a number of attributes of each QDIA type that could make it a good choice for a plan, as shown in table 1.

Even though some attributes are unique to a single QDIA type, the combination of features that each QDIA type contains can affect a plan sponsor's choice. Stakeholders we interviewed and plan sponsors responding to our questionnaire highlighted specific reasons that could make a QDIA type an appropriate choice for a plan.

Table 1. A Comparison of Attributes Associated with Each Qualified Default Investment Alternative (QDIA)

Theme	Attributes	Balanced funds	Off-the-shelf target-date funds	Custom target-date funds	Managed accounts
Design simplicity	Easy to implement	√	√		
	Design easy to communicate to participants	√	√		
	"One-size-fits-all" design	√			
Investment performance	Access to best-in-class managers and funds			√	
	Builds on underlying core investments			√	√
Fiduciary protection	Perceived as low cost	√	√	[a]	[a]
	Allows performance comparisons within QDIA type	√	√		
	Easy to monitor	√		√	√
	Allows partial transfer of fiduciary responsibility				√
Customization	Asset allocations change as participants age		√	√	√
	QDIA portfolios can be tailored to individual participant				√[b]
	QDIA portfolios customized to plan features			√	
	Uses participant information to assign portfolios				√
	Focus on participant's retirement goals				√

Source: GAO analysis based on stakeholder interviews and plan sponsor responses to GAO's questionnaire. | GAO-15-578

[a] While many sponsors and stakeholders said that the cost of custom target-date funds and managed accounts is high, others stated that this is not necessarily the case. For example, sponsors with large plans may achieve economies of scale that can significantly lower the costs of the QDIA product or service. In addition, higher returns achieved by these QDIA types could offset their higher cost. However, the customized nature of these QDIA types and the lack of comparable performance data make it difficult to determine how the net costs for managed accounts compare with net costs of other QDIA types.

[b] DOL regulations require that funds be allocated among investment alternatives available under the plan. 29 C.F.R. § 2550.404c-5(e)(4)(iii). As a result, the ability of a managed account provider to individualize a QDIA participant account may depend on the variety of asset classes available under the plan. Some managed account providers told us that they either advise or require a plan to be adequately diversified.

- **Off-the-shelf TDFs:** Several stakeholders stated that plan sponsors generally selected off-the shelf TDFs because they are a conceptually simple, low-cost product that provides diversification and dynamic asset allocation throughout a participant's career. Some plan sponsors responding to our questionnaire who selected off-the-shelf TDFs as QDIA said that these products had beneficial characteristics, such as being tailored for a workforce that spanned diverse age groups, having a simple design, providing age-based asset allocations at a low cost, and creating appropriate retirement outcomes for participants who had little interest in investing and tended not to change their investment selections over time.
- **Custom TDFs:** Stakeholders stated that plan sponsors generally selected custom TDFs because these products provide plan sponsors with a more hands-on approach to investment management. For example, three stakeholders noted that, unlike off-the-shelf TDFs, custom TDFs allow sponsors to select best-in-class asset management to build a TDF series that meets the needs of the plan.[31] A plan sponsor responding to our questionnaire who selected a custom TDF as QDIA told us that her plan set out to develop a custom target-date glide path using plan specific demographic information and the current plan investment fund managers. As part of this process, a service provider selected a glide path that provided the best return for risk, based on participant demographics, income needs, and behavioral investment patterns.
- **Balanced funds:** Several stakeholders indicated that plan sponsors generally selected these funds for their simple design, which makes them easy to understand, manage, and monitor. Stakeholders noted that, in many cases, balanced funds had been in a plan's investment lineup for years and were familiar to sponsors and participants. Some plan sponsors responding to our questionnaire who selected balanced funds as QDIA said that these products had beneficial characteristics, such as having a simple design, low costs, asset diversification, and a proven investment approach with a performance track record.
- **Managed accounts:** Several stakeholders stated that plan sponsors generally selected managed accounts because they offered the greatest level of fiduciary protection among QDIA types and aligned with participants' unique characteristics or workforce demographics, such

as (1) having been grandfathered into a plan, (2) having pension benefits or deferred compensation, or (3) being salaried or hourly wage earners. Some stakeholders noted that sponsors also preferred that managed account providers have full discretion over participant portfolios being managed in a QDIA and viewed managed accounts as a retirement planning tool with the long-term focus on getting participants retirement income for life. Two stakeholders also noted that plan sponsors can input additional employee data to help managed account providers customize participant portfolios. Two plan sponsors responding to our questionnaire who selected a managed account as a QDIA said that managed accounts had beneficial characteristics, such as (1) being appropriate for all employees (including mid-career hires who may have assets outside the plan), (2) offering the best asset diversification, and (3) having the ability to take into account an employee's risk tolerance as well as age. In addition, one respondent with a managed account QDIA said that managed accounts had a superior level of customization that could lead to better participant outcomes, while another respondent indicated that managed account services are offered at costs competitive to other available investment advice services.

Exercising due diligence when selecting a QDIA type that aligns with a plan's objectives can involve a complex process with many steps.[32] Several stakeholders identified additional factors beyond the favorable attributes of each QDIA type that can influence a plan sponsor's QDIA considerations, such as sponsor preferences, plan circumstances, and environmental conditions. For example, one stakeholder noted that a plan sponsor can reject a consultant recommendation and select an investment option already in the plan or choose a QDIA frequently used among peers. Other stakeholders said that a sponsor may also decide against selecting a QDIA to avoid any risk of having to assume fiduciary responsibility if the investment does not perform well. Changes in the environment in which a plan is situated, such as a plan merger or court decision, could lead a sponsor to change a plan's QDIA, according to stakeholders.[33] As shown in figure 3, stakeholders identified how a combination of plan sponsor's perceptions, plan circumstances, and environmental factors can influence how a plan sponsor approaches QDIA selection and the type of QDIA selected.

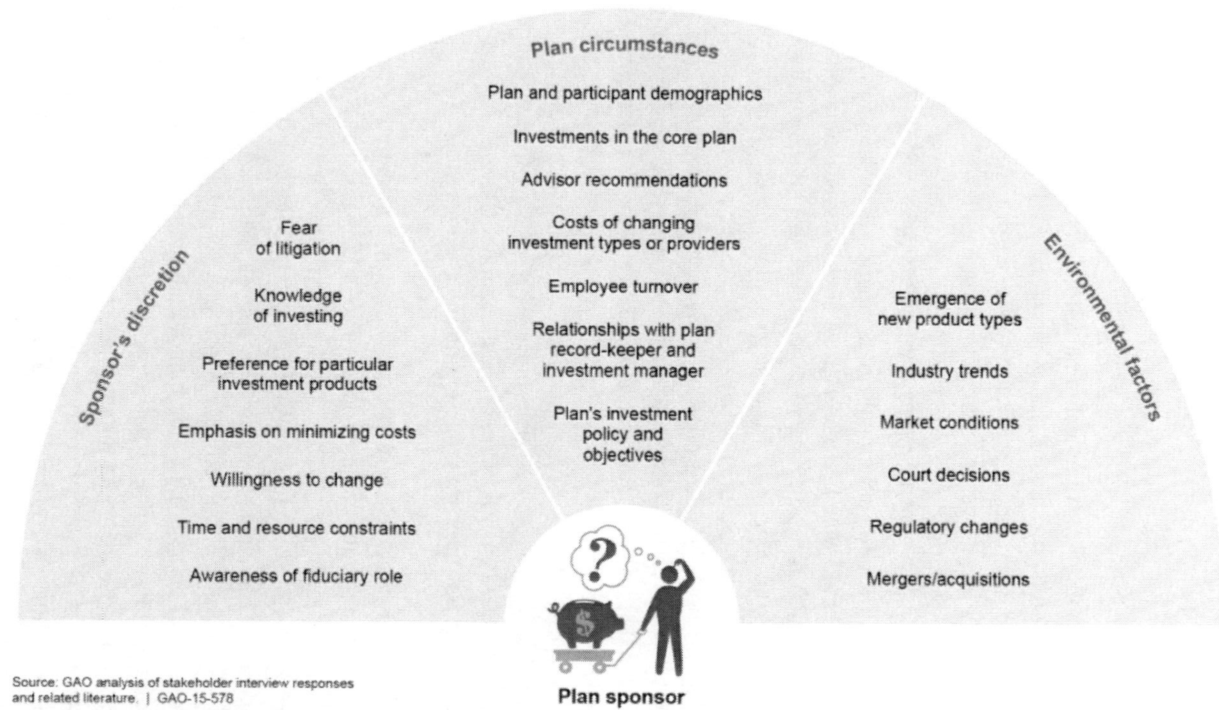

Source: GAO analysis of stakeholder interview responses and related literature. | GAO-15-578

Figure 3. Select Factors That Stakeholders Said Might Influence a Plan Sponsor's Default Investment Selection.

Plan Sponsors Consider Multiple Factors When Monitoring Default Investments, and Results Depend on Plan-Specific Considerations

Plan sponsors responding to our questionnaire told us that they performed periodic monitoring of plan investments, including any default investments, by conducting quantitative and qualitative analysis to ensure the investments aligned with the plan's objectives and investment strategies. According to DOL officials, a plan sponsor should periodically compare the performance of its investment options, including its QDIA, against other similar investment products and against applicable performance benchmarks. Plan sponsors stated that they compared different quantitative metrics, such as investment returns, risks, and costs for the QDIA against comparison groups or indices, commonly across 1-, 3-, and 5-year time periods. For example, plan sponsors told us that they examined: (1) investment returns on an absolute basis, as well as relative to the performance of comparison groups or other relevant benchmarks; (2) volatility of investment returns or returns adjusted for risk; and (3) the percentage of assets deducted for fund expenses, sales fees, or other charges associated with the investment.

Plan sponsors told us that they also examined several different qualitative metrics when monitoring a QDIA to determine whether significant changes had occurred since the QDIA was selected or last examined.[34]

For example, sponsors stated that they monitored changes in:

- **Plan characteristics:** With respect to TDFs and managed accounts, DOL regulations require plan sponsors to take participant age into account when selecting a QDIA that has portfolios that become less risky as the participant ages.[35] With respect to balanced funds, plan sponsors are required to consider the age of plan participants as a whole.[36] An employer with an older workforce might reconsider using a balanced fund as a QDIA if the plan's demographics changed by a significant number of younger participants enrolling in the plan. Some plan sponsors also consider other plan characteristics, such as the existence of a DB plan or average job tenure, in determining the suitability of their QDIA, but DOL regulations do not require them to do so.[37] Regardless of whether a sponsor only considered age or additional plan characteristics when the QDIA was selected, substantial changes in any of these factors could determine whether the QDIA continued to be a suitable investment.

- **Plan investment policies and objectives:** Plan sponsors reported that they monitored how well a QDIA aligned with the plan investment policies and objectives. For example, a plan sponsor stated that the plan's policy statement required investments not meeting pre-established benchmarks for 2 consecutive quarters to be placed on a watch list for more frequent in-depth monitoring.[38] Similarly, because a plan's investment objectives can change over time, plan sponsors monitor how well the QDIA aligns with new objectives. For example, one plan sponsor responding to our questionnaire said that his plan changed from an actively managed QDIA to a QDIA that consisted of index funds—passively managed products with the objective of approximating the same return as particular market indices (such as the S&P 500)—in order to align the QDIA investment strategy with the passive savings approach of defaulted participants.[39]
- **Service providers:** Plan sponsors stated that they monitored service provider adherence to the plan's investment management strategy. For example, plan sponsors stated that they examined the extent to which the provider faithfully implemented the investment strategy outlined in the QDIA's fund prospectus by, for example, tracking the performance of an index fund relative to that of the market index it tracked. One plan sponsor responding to our questionnaire said changes in fund management or investment processes would cause him to place the fund on a watch list and ask the plan's investment consultant to engage in additional discussions with the fund managers. Other sponsors stated they monitored fee structures, portfolio composition, asset allocations, and investment diversification, as well as the service provider's qualifications.

Default Investment Type and Resource Availability Can Affect Plan Sponsors' Monitoring Efforts

Plan sponsors responding to our questionnaire and stakeholders we interviewed stated that the structure and features of each QDIA type affects how they monitor them. For example, plan sponsors and stakeholders told us that quantitative performance data across similar investments varied by QDIA type, with balanced funds and off-the-shelf TDFs having more data with which to compare peer funds and benchmarks than custom TDFs and managed accounts. Some sponsors noted that the fixed asset allocation of balanced funds facilitated easy comparisons of the QDIA's returns, risks, and costs against other individual balanced funds, a balanced fund peer group, or other relevant benchmarks. A TDF's glide path, on the other hand, required plan sponsors to monitor the performance of the entire target-date series as well as each of the individual funds within it. They stated that the variation in glide paths among target-date series made it difficult for the sponsor to identify peer TDFs (or appropriate benchmarks) with similar objectives, asset allocations, and risk attributes.[40] In contrast, plan sponsors with a managed account reported that they monitor only the managed account provider to ensure that the contracted services are being provided rather than considering investment performance. Plan sponsors are generally unable to compare managed account services across providers because of a lack of consistent performance information;[41] however, plan sponsors with managed accounts told us that they periodically reviewed the performance of their QDIA.

The availability of resources and expertise devoted to investment monitoring can affect the extent of QDIA monitoring that plan sponsors can conduct.[42] Stakeholders we interviewed generally said that small plan sponsors typically have fewer resources to devote to more in-depth investment analysis and often rely on outside advisors, while large plans often have in-house expertise and resources to devote to conducting more in-depth investment analysis.[43] Consequently, according to stakeholders, small plan sponsors are more likely to rely on simple peer- relative return or fee comparisons, while large plan sponsors are more likely to have access to sophisticated analytics and perform more in-depth analysis. Some plan sponsors responding to our questionnaire and stakeholders we interviewed stated that, in addition to monitoring general performance metrics, a sponsor may examine asset allocations and glide paths, underlying assets of investments, and associated fund managers and investment strategy. Table 2 shows examples of some activities that plan sponsors used when performing more in-depth analysis.

Plan Circumstances Dictate Sponsors' Responses to Monitoring

Plan circumstances affect a sponsor's response to their periodic QDIA monitoring. According to DOL officials, in cases where a plan's objectives in choosing a particular investment are no longer being met due to a fund's investment fee structure, investment strategy, or management team change, it may be necessary for a plan sponsor to consider replacing the investment. Whereas plan sponsors reported generally retaining QDIAs that meet performance expectations, a sponsor's decision to change course can depend on circumstances specific to the plan if monitoring indicates that a QDIA may no longer be suitable for the plan. For example, one sponsor stated that his plan was in the process of changing the QDIA to a publicly-traded TDF because they thought it would provide better transparency for participants. Another plan sponsor said his plan would consider changing a QDIA that was performing well if another option in the marketplace appeared to better serve plan participants. Another sponsor said that the popularity of TDFs as QDIAs among peers in the marketplace led his plan to change the QDIA to a TDF. As shown in table 3, changes to a plan's QDIA can range from minor modifications to comprehensive changes in a QDIA investment's features, options, provider, or even type.

Table 2. Types of Analysis Sponsors and Stakeholders Reported Conducting When Monitoring a Plan's Qualified Default Investment Alternative

Analysis conducted	Examples of activities performed
Examine asset allocation and glide paths[a]	Determine whether the asset allocation and glide path as set forth in the fund prospectus or service agreement have been adhered to for the monitoring period. Compare the performance of investment alternatives by identifying those products or services that have the same or similar asset allocation and glide path.
Examine underlying assets[b]	Examine performance of the underlying investment products or services at the sub-asset class, such as looking at technology stocks within the overall stock asset class, or individual stocks or bonds comprising the asset class. For each sub-asset or individual security examined, monitor the investment managers and determine whether the investment strategy as outlined in the fund prospectus have been adhered to for the monitoring period.

Source: GAO interviews with plan sponsors and stakeholders and analysis of DOL and industry publications | GAO-15-578

[a] Balanced funds generally have a fixed asset allocation so their glide paths, to the extent that they can be said to have one, go neither up nor down but remain constant over time.

[b] Examining underlying assets is a complex process, because three funds with similar equity and fixed-income allocations may use different stocks and bonds, each with varying levels of risk that can affect performance and costs. Furthermore, a sponsor may need to monitor each underlying fund, which likely has separate investment strategies and managers that can vary.

Table 3. Changes Plan Sponsors Can Make to a Plan's Qualified Default Investment Alternative (QDIA)

Type of change	Description	Examples
Change investment features	This change involves modifications to an existing investment used as a QDIA. Features that could be modified include the investment strategy, asset allocation, glide path, risk profile, and customization, among others.	A plan sponsor with a custom TDF that wants to adjust its risk exposure may change its asset allocation or glide path accordingly. A plan sponsor with a managed account that wants to enhance its account customization may provide additional information about defaulted participants to the provider so that it can be considered in the portfolio allocation decisions.
Change investment options	This change involves making adjustments to the investments that make up a plan's QDIA and could include modifying the plan's investment options. (This type of change may be unavailable to sponsors who use a QDIA made up of proprietary funds.)	A plan sponsor could decide to incorporate additional asset classes (e.g., alternative investments, real estate, etc.) into the investment menu. A plan sponsor that wants the ability to include non-proprietary funds from any provider may change to an approach that allows them to customize the underlying assets. A plan sponsor with a QDIA made up of proprietary funds wanting to adopt a custom TDF with "best-in-class" funds for all asset classes will most likely need to change to a non-proprietary approach that allows use of funds from other providers.
Change investment fund or service provider	This change involves replacing the provider of an existing QDIA with another while maintaining the same type of QDIA.	A plan sponsor with a balanced fund from one company could choose another balanced fund with similar allocation, objectives and risk characteristics from another company. For investment management services, such as managed accounts, the change would similarly replace one provider with another.

Type of change	Description	Examples
Change QDIA type	This change involves replacing an existing QDIA with another type of QDIA. Changing a QDIA type can also include modifications to any of the above categories.	A plan could change their QDIA from a passively managed proprietary balanced fund to an actively managed custom TDF. Such a change would involve not only changing the QDIA type, but also the plan investment architecture and the investment strategy. The change could also involve a change to the provider.

Source: GAO analysis of interviews with plan sponsors and industry publications. | GAO-15-578

Plan sponsors responding to our questionnaire and stakeholders we interviewed stated that after an extensive QDIA selection process, sponsors may be reluctant to make changes to the investment due to cost considerations, existing service provider arrangements, and fiduciary concerns.

- **Cost:** Stakeholders noted that changing a QDIA can be costly and may require considerable time and resources. For example, one stakeholder noted that QDIA changes require plan sponsors to notify participants, explaining the reasons for any changes and how it will affect their accounts. Sponsors said that the significant time and cost needed to implement a change could outweigh any perceived short-term benefit. One stakeholder noted that a plan sponsor who changes a QDIA for underperformance could find the plan in the same situation should the replacement QDIA underperform within a few years.
- **Existing service provider arrangements:** A plan sponsor's existing relationship with a service provider can limit plan sponsors' access to certain QDIA types and may make it challenging to change a QDIA. For example, a sponsor using a proprietary off-the-shelf TDF as a QDIA has limited options to change the QDIA if funds in the TDF series (or underlying funds) perform below expectations. Stakeholders stated that, in cases where a sponsor had negotiated reduced fees for using a certain QDIA, a change of QDIA could jeopardize the arrangement and increase the costs for managing or administering the investments. Similarly, a plan sponsor deciding to use a managed account as its QDIA may find that the record keeper had not partnered with a managed account provider, leaving the sponsor to either select

a different QDIA or change record keepers—both options that plan sponsors cited as highly disruptive and costly.

- **Fiduciary concerns:** Plan sponsors and stakeholders stated that any change to a QDIA could expose sponsors to additional fiduciary liability. One plan sponsor stated that fear of potential litigation led the plan's investment committee to decide against changing a QDIA, even though the committee believed that initial selection decisions had been prudent and participants would be better served by the change.

PLAN SPONSORS CITE REGULATORY UNCERTAINTY, EXTENT OF FIDUCIARY PROTECTION, AND ABILITY TO ADOPT INNOVATIVE PRODUCTS AS SIGNIFICANT CHALLENGES

Stakeholders Noted That Information Provided by DOL on Consideration of Participant Demographics Is Unclear and Difficult for Some Plan Sponsors to Follow

Stakeholders we interviewed generally said that plan sponsors had particular difficulty understanding how to account for plan demographics when selecting a QDIA. Federal agencies are generally required to draft regulations that are easy to understand with the goal of minimizing uncertainty and potential litigation.[44] DOL's regulations prescribe, and the preamble accompanying its publication discuss, one specific demographic characteristic—ages of the participants—that sponsors must always consider when making their QDIA selections, and the regulations prescribe two sets of criteria for sponsors to apply when considering the ages of plan participants:

1. sponsors considering a TDF or managed account service as a QDIA should consider a product or service that includes a mix of equity and fixed income allocations *"based on the participant's age, target retirement date (such as normal retirement age under the plan) or life expectancy."* [45]
2. sponsors considering a balanced fund as a QDIA *"are not required to take into account the age of an individual participant,"* [46] but rather *"focus on the participant population as a whole."* [47]

The QDIA type that a sponsor selects based on these age determinations can alter the asset allocation of QDIA participant accounts and how the allocation may change over time. For example, a 50-year old QDIA participant could end up in a much different investment portfolio in a balanced fund than he or she would in a managed account, as shown in figure 4.

In connection with prior work, stakeholders stated that age should not be the sole determinant for whether a QDIA met the needs of affected participants and recommended that DOL amend the QDIA regulations to require fiduciaries to document whether they had considered participant characteristics other than age when choosing a QDIA.[48] DOL disagreed with this recommendation, noting that its intent in requiring the consideration of one factor—age—was to give plan sponsors certainty that they were complying with the regulations and that nothing in the regulations precluded the consideration of other factors. However, DOL agreed that it may be appropriate for a fiduciary to consider other characteristics and indicated that it would include such considerations in its guidance to plan fiduciaries, which it did in a 2013 publication designed to assist plan fiduciaries in selecting a TDF.[49]

Stakeholders we interviewed generally said that plan sponsors were unsure of which population of participants they should consider when making their QDIA selections. Some stakeholders noted that sponsors did not know whether they should consider the demographics of (1) all potential and existing plan participants together, (2) the plan as a whole, or (3) only the demographics of those participants defaulted into—or likely to be defaulted into—the plan's QDIA. Other sponsors responding to our questionnaire noted that, while sponsors could determine the average age of the plan as a whole, they could not determine the ages of participants unlikely to direct their investments and thus be in need of a QDIA. One sponsor suggested that, even with the DOL regulations, sponsors would benefit from knowing how other plans considered participant demographics. Sponsors selecting managed accounts as a QDIA do not face this issue because the managed account providers consider each participant's age regardless of whether the participant opted-in to the service or were defaulted into the service by a plan sponsor.

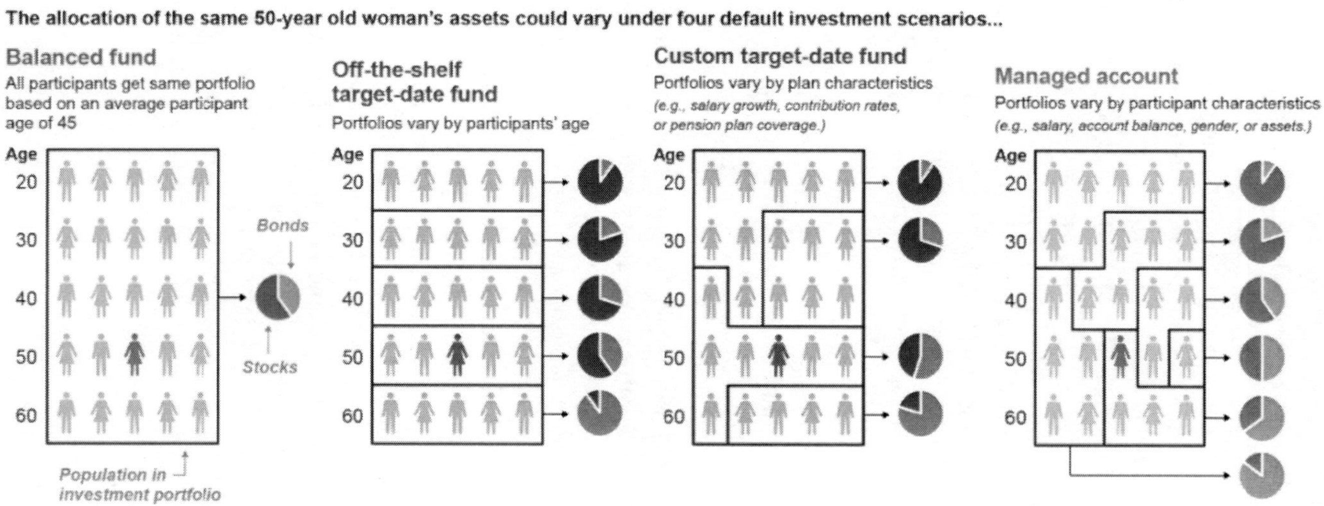

Source: GAO analysis of industry descriptions of the features of Qualified Default Investment Alternatives (QDIA). | GAO-15-578

Figure 4. Illustration of How Plan Sponsors Might Consider Age When Determining Asset Allocation Strategies for Qualified Default Investment Alternative (QDIA) Participants, by QDIA Type.

Plan sponsors responding to our questionnaire also stated that it was difficult to find a QDIA that best fit the age range or distribution of a plan's participant population. For example, more than half of the plan sponsors responding to our questionnaire indicated that it was challenging to select a QDIA that best fit all plan participants. Two plan sponsors noted that they were unsure how to apply the DOL regulations to plans with varied demographic profiles, making it difficult to select a single fund as a QDIA. One sponsor stated that many QDIA models rely on a hypothetical average participant and result in a portfolio, which by definition is unlikely to match the investment needs of other plan participants. Another sponsor noted that for plans in which participants tend to retire at age 55 or at age 69, an off-the-shelf TDF that assumes a retirement age of 65 may not match a plan's demographics. Other sponsors stated that plan demographics were neither uniform nor constant over time, making it difficult to identify a QDIA that would meet the needs of plan participants on a long-term basis. Some sponsors stated that it was difficult to select a TDF series that applied to a plan's age distribution. For example, one sponsor noted that his plan had "barbell demographics"—with clusters of participants at each end of the age spectrum and few in between— making it difficult to find an off-the-shelf TDF series, which can include funds for many age groups, to fit the plan. Another sponsor noted that some plans may have an overly narrow age demographic—young or old—that made the adoption of an entire TDF series unnecessary and expensive.

Some plan sponsors responding to our questionnaire stated that they had particular difficulty applying the DOL regulations when selecting a balanced fund and that regulatory uncertainty made it less likely that sponsors would adopt this QDIA type. The DOL regulations state that when considering a balanced fund as a QDIA, a sponsor must determine a level of risk that is appropriate for all affected participants,[50] but DOL noted when it published the final regulations that an appropriate level of risk is unlikely to be optimal for all participants.[51] Although DOL recognized this as one disadvantage of balanced funds, DOL also identified several advantages—balanced funds are simpler, less expensive, and easier to explain and understand than the other QDIA types—and noted that these advantages may sometimes outweigh the potential disadvantage of more customized risk levels offered in the other QDIA types. Two stakeholders noted that, without additional information about a participant's financial situation outside of the plan, a plan sponsor could have insufficient information to determine which asset allocation provided an appropriate level of risk. Others stated that the regulations do not provide sponsors with sufficient guidance to choose a balanced fund.

Some plan sponsors also may have concerns about how to address changing demographics in a plan that uses a balanced fund as a QDIA, according to stakeholders. For example, one stakeholder noted that it was unclear what a sponsor should do if plan demographics change, how a sponsor would monitor those changes, and how quickly a sponsor would need to respond to those changes to meet regulatory requirements. This stakeholder also noted that the requirement to consider age in the context of the plan as a whole discourages the use of balanced funds as QDIAs because it would require a sponsor to track and react to demographic changes, making potential for liability high. Changes in the age of the plan's participants can also change the extent to which a QDIA aligns with the average participant's retirement needs. Another stakeholder noted there is a need to be sensitive to the possibility that two participants could be the same age but have different investment strategies, or conversely, share the same investment strategy at different ages.

Some Plan Sponsors Are Unsure of the Extent of Fiduciary Protection

Stakeholders we interviewed generally said that plan sponsors selected a QDIA specifically for the additional fiduciary protection it provided under DOL's safe harbor. Despite the requirement that regulations be easy to understand with the goal of minimizing uncertainty and potential litigation, some sponsors were unsure of the extent of this protection or whether each QDIA type provided the same level of protection. For example, more than half of the 227 plan sponsors responding to our questionnaire indicated that the three QDIA types did not offer the same fiduciary protection, or they said that they did not know or had no basis to judge. Although DOL indicated when it published its final regulations that "[a]s long as a plan fiduciary selects any of the qualified default investment alternatives, and otherwise complies with the conditions of the rule, the plan fiduciary will obtain the fiduciary relief described in the rule,"[52] some sponsors stated that they believed the level of fiduciary protection that each QDIA type provided was not equal. Plan sponsors shared a general perception that certain QDIA types offered greater fiduciary protection than others, but they offered divergent opinions on which type or design provided the most protection.

Despite the stated status of the QDIA as a safe harbor, some plan sponsors who adopted a QDIA described what they perceived to be a sliding scale of fiduciary protection ranging from "one-size-fits-all" balanced funds to custom TDFs and managed account services; however, they offered no consensus on which QDIA types offered the greatest protection. One sponsor we interviewed and three sponsors who responded to our questionnaire reported that they did not adopt a QDIA. Of this group, two reported having difficulty seeing the advantage in assuming more risk for the possibility of achieving better retirement outcomes for participants who choose not to direct their investments and two indicated that they believed requiring participants to make an investment election provided the best fiduciary protection. Plan sponsors' views of fiduciary protection varied depending on the importance they placed on the QDIA design and costs.

- **Design:** Some plan sponsors indicated that the level of fiduciary protection could vary depending on the complexity of the QDIA design. Some sponsors expressed the belief that the simple design of balanced funds and off-the-shelf TDFs—which apply one or similar investment strategies to large groups of participants—provided more fiduciary protection. Other sponsors viewed the design simplicity of these QDIA types as a potential liability and preferred what they perceived to be the added protection of a customized QDIA design. For example, two stakeholders said that sponsors viewed the ability of the more complex customized QDIA types, such as managed accounts, to address specific plan or individual participant objectives helped reduce their fiduciary liability.[53]
- **Costs:** Some plan sponsors said that they believed the level of fiduciary protection could vary depending on the costs associated with the QDIA type. Some sponsors selecting balanced funds or off-the-shelf TDFs said that, by selecting a low-cost QDIA option and closely monitoring fees, they felt that they could demonstrate that they acted in the best interests of participants. Others noted that costs alone should not be the determining factor and that sponsors with more customized QDIAs, such as custom TDFs, obtained greater fiduciary protection by tailoring the QDIA to meet the needs of the plan and participants. For example, one stakeholder noted that, unlike off-the-shelf products, custom TDFs can include more diversified investments, such as hedge funds, commodities, and other asset classes, that can provide greater diversification and inflation

protection. Two sponsors using a managed account QDIA noted that managed accounts can take into account a participant's extended investment portfolio beyond the 401(k) plan and thereby provide an individualized account that aligns with a participant's financial circumstances. In addition, by serving as a co-fiduciary, a managed account provider told us that he offered sponsors an added layer of protection by assuming responsibility and discretion for managing plan investments. In addition, one managed account provider noted that off-the-shelf TDFs, often seen as a low-cost option, can cost more than some managed account services, which have the ability to use available participant information to place participant contributions into an account that is both age- and risk-appropriate.

Stakeholders we interviewed generally said that some plan sponsors were unsure whether the QDIA safe harbor extended to the re-enrollment of participants—a process by which sponsors may re-invest all of a participant's existing assets in a plan's QDIA unless the participant opts out.[54] The final DOL regulations and the preamble that accompanied their publication do not explicitly refer to re-enrollment, but the preamble describes three circumstances in which fiduciary relief may be available under the regulations to plan sponsors who, in effect, re-enroll participants: (1) the failure of a participant to provide investment direction following the elimination of an investment alternative from the plan[55] or a change in service provider, (2) failure of a participant to provide investment direction following a rollover from another plan,[56] and (3) any other failure of a participant to provide investment instruction. In some cases, plan sponsors have indicated that they use re-enrollment in an attempt to improve the investment outcomes for participants who the sponsor believes have made poor investment decisions. Some viewed this process as controversial and contrary to the purpose of a self-directed account. DOL officials told us they fashioned the QDIA regulation to cover a variety of circumstances in which participants are given the opportunity to direct their investments, but do not do so. They also noted that some sponsors relied on the regulation to justify re-enrollment and that at least one court has held that the regulations covered re- enrollment, as long as conditions in the regulations are met.[57] However, some sponsors said that they worried about exposing themselves to potential liability considering that the re-enrollment process could effectively override participants' investment elections by placing assets in an investment that a participant specifically did not select. A suboptimal choice of QDIA could have long-lasting negative effects on participants' retirement savings if the choice does not align with a participant's needs. One stakeholder noted that more sponsors would be inclined to implement re-enrollment to improve participant outcomes if DOL confirmed that re-enrollment was a reasonable application of the QDIA rules and provided examples of how sponsors should implement re- enrollment.

Some Plan Sponsors Are Unsure Whether Regulations Allow for the Adoption of Innovative Solutions

Stakeholders we interviewed generally said that some sponsors would like to incorporate other retirement features, such as annuitization,[58] in their plan's QDIA to improve retirement outcomes for participants; however, they were unsure whether such products would qualify for fiduciary protection. One stakeholder stated that one of the benefits of DB plans is the provision of a lifetime annuity upon retirement and that replicating this feature in the DC plan context warranted further attention. Another stakeholder noted that it was important for participants invested in a QDIA for an entire career to have some means to accrue lifetime retirement income. Without such a plan feature, another stakeholder noted, participants defaulted into a QDIA would likely be at a disadvantage compared to those with accrued lifetime retirement income, when faced with the decision about what to do with their accumulated assets at retirement.

DOL officials said that they anticipated and encouraged innovation in the plan investment marketplace, including lifetime retirement income features. In the preamble to the final QDIA regulations, DOL indicated that the regulations are sufficiently flexible to accommodate future innovations and developments in retirement products. Specifically, DOL officials noted that the examples were included solely for the purpose of providing guidance as to what might be within the defined categories and were not intended in any way to limit the application of the QDIA regulations to other products. In 2014, DOL outlined specific conditions under which a TDF series could incorporate some form of deferred annuity contract and remain a QDIA.[59] One plan sponsor said that until sponsors were certain that other products qualified for QDIA protection, they were unlikely to deviate from strict adherence to the safe harbor conditions or consider products other than the three named QDIA types. However, the regulations indicate that the QDIAs are not the exclusive means by which a plan fiduciary may satisfy plan responsibilities respecting the investment of participant assets of their behalf.[60]

Several stakeholders stated that the current QDIA types require greater scrutiny to ensure that they will lead to better default investments. For example, one stakeholder stated that QDIAs can be improved to mitigate the down-side risk of TDFs and provide participants with lifetime retirement income.[61] Another stakeholder noted that no QDIA type provides explicit inflation protection, saying that QDIAs should include an inflation-indexed investment to protect inattentive participants and beneficiaries. One stakeholder said that the regulations should allow flexibility for more hybrid approaches to a plan's QDIA, such as multiple plan QDIAs to cater to different segments of plan populations.[62] However, this stakeholder concluded that product developers would be unlikely to take initiative to create new QDIA products and services as long as uncertainty in the regulations persists.

CONCLUSION

QDIAs have been a significant development for increasing worker participation in defined contribution plans since they were first authorized under PPA. DOL's safe harbor has encouraged many plan sponsors to adopt automatic enrollment policies and invest the assets of defaulted participants into investments they have deemed appropriate for long-term retirement savings. While PPA encouraged the adoption of QDIAs through the creation of safe harbor plan designs, some plan sponsors find the final DOL regulations to be unclear, especially with regard to the consideration of participant ages when selecting a QDIA, the extent of fiduciary protection, and the flexibility to allow innovations in QDIA products. This lack of clarity could lead some plan sponsors to make suboptimal choices when selecting a plan's default investment and could have long-lasting negative effects on participants' retirement savings.

As a consequence, plan sponsors remain concerned about their liability and are looking for additional clarification of existing laws and regulations. Without a better understanding of the requirements, plan sponsors— including those that have already adopted a QDIA—face difficulties trying to balance participant safeguards with solutions that can help them establish and sustain financially secure retirement plans for their employees.

Recommendation for Executive Action

To encourage plan sponsors to continue efforts to improve plan participation and overall retirement savings through the use of QDIAs, we recommend that the Secretary of Labor direct the Assistant Secretary for the Employee Benefits Security Administration to assess the challenges that plan sponsors and stakeholders reported, including the extent to which these challenges can be addressed, and implement corrective actions through clarifying guidance or regulations, as appropriate.

Agency Comments

We provided a draft of this product to the Department of Labor for review and comment. In its written comments DOL generally concurred with our findings and recommendation. In its comments, DOL officials stated that they would review the challenges that GAO reported, consider how best to assess those challenges, and determine whether additional actions would be beneficial to stakeholders. DOL also provided technical comments that were incorporated, as appropriate.

Sincerely yours,

Charles A. Jeszeck, Director
Education, Workforce, and Income Security Issues

Appendix I: Objectives, Scope, and Methodology

The objectives for this study were to determine: (1) which options plan sponsors selected as QDIAs and why; (2) how plan sponsors monitor their QDIA selections; and (3) what challenges, if any, plan sponsors report facing when adopting a QDIA for their plan.

Overall Methodology

Each of the engagement's three researchable objectives required us to gain the insights of plan sponsors of 401(k)-type plans. For all objectives, we reviewed relevant federal laws, regulations, and guidance on the use of QDIAs in 401(k)-type plans. To learn about the issues facing sponsors when selecting and monitoring a QDIA, we interviewed 96 stakeholders knowledgeable of the topic of QDIA use—including plan sponsors, plan sponsor advocates; plan service providers, plan consultants, plan record keepers, investment managers, and managed account providers; participant advocates; and academicians—who provided us with a broad range of perspectives on issues surrounding the use of QDIAs. In each interview, we solicited names of additional stakeholders to interview until we had coverage of a broad range of perspectives.

To determine the prevalence of default investment use in DC plans, we examined annual data for the years 2009 through 2013 on private-sector DC plans included in (1) DOL's Form 5500 database that identified the number of plans that reported having automatic enrollment and default investments and (2) selected industry surveys of plan sponsors that identified types of default investments that plan sponsors used.

To better understand the experiences of plan sponsors with respect to QDIA selection and monitoring efforts, we developed a web-based questionnaire that was publicized with the assistance of several professional organizations whose memberships included plan sponsors and others who act as plan fiduciaries.

To better understand the types of performance information that plan sponsors could use to monitor the three QDIA types—target-date funds, balanced funds, and managed accounts—we analyzed available financial market data on target-date funds and balanced funds for a number of returns, risk, and cost metrics for different time periods. For managed accounts, we also reviewed sample performance reports obtained from selected providers.

All data collected through these methods are nongeneralizable and reflect the views and experiences of the respondents and not the entire population of employer-sponsored 401(k)-type plans. However, we believe the insights gained through these methods produced valuable information to better understand the effect of the QDIA regulations on selected plan sponsors.

Industry Surveys

Because there are no nationally representative data on the universe of 401(k) plan sponsors' default investment selections, we used data from three industry surveys that were publicly accessible and provided consistent annual data on default investment use for the most consecutive years, from 2009 through 2013. Given that our focus was the prevalence of QDIA use among plan sponsors, we combined all other categories of non-QDIA default investment vehicles that plan sponsors listed in the surveys. We assessed the reliability of the survey data from the three surveys by ensuring consistency of (1) data reporting and identifying the number of respondents, (2) the variation of plan sizes, and (3) the industry sectors represented in each survey. We found these data to be sufficiently reliable when aggregated, as we did in this product. The survey results, while the best available data, are not generalizable to the universe of DC plans. See below for additional information on the survey respondents in the most recent year that we used.

- **Survey A:** From late June through early September 2013, an industry organization, PLANSPONSOR, conducted a survey of DC plan sponsors and received 5,342 usable responses.[63] Employers that participated in the survey represented a broad variety of U.S. industries and plan sizes. About 71 percent of the 5,342 respondents had less than $50 million, 23 percent had between $50 million and $1 billion, and 6 percent had more than $1 billion in plan assets.
- **Survey B:** In the fall of 2013, a second industry organization, Callan Investments Institute, conducted an online survey of DC plans, and 107 sponsor responses were incorporated in the results.[64] Survey respondents represented a wide range of industries and plan sizes, with the top three industries represented being government (18 percent), manufacturing (14 percent), and technology (11 percent). About 6 percent of the 107 respondents had less than $50 million, 36 percent had between $50 million and $1 billion, and 58 percent had more than $1 billion in plan assets.
- **Survey C:** In 2013 and early 2014, a third industry organization, Deloitte, conducted an online survey of DC plans, collecting data from 265 plan sponsors.[65] Employers that participated in the survey represent a comprehensive range of industries and employer sizes, with the top three represented industry sectors being manufacturing (22 percent), consumer business and transportation (20 percent), and

financial services and insurance (17 percent). About 38 percent of the 209 plan respondents who provided information on plan assets had less than $50 million, 43 percent had between $50 million and $1 billion, and 19 percent had more than $1 billion in plan assets.

GAO Questionnaire

To better understand the experiences of plan sponsors with respect to QDIA selection and monitoring efforts, we developed a web-based questionnaire that was publicized with the assistance of four professional organizations—PLANSPONSOR, National Association of Plan Advisors, Plan Sponsor Council of America, and the Stable Value Investment Association—whose memberships included plan sponsors or others who serve as plan fiduciaries. As part of our general interview process, we met and interviewed representatives of several industry groups that had large and diverse memberships of plan sponsors. Four groups agreed to publicize our questionnaire in their communications to group members. Each group publicized the questionnaire and provided their members with a link to access it directly. The web-based questionnaire remained open from October 1, 2014, through January 30, 2015. When the questionnaire closed, we had collected responses from 227 plan sponsors. We analyzed the questionnaire responses as a group and then by QDIA type and plan size. Of these respondents, 40 reported that they had selected a balanced fund, 14 had selected a professionally managed account, 170 had selected a TDF as QDIA, and 3 respondents had selected a plan default investment that was not a QDIA. Respondents were distributed across all plan sizes, defined both by the number of participants and by volume of assets under management. We also followed up with 55 respondents who voluntarily provided their contact information.

To gather more granular anecdotal detail on sponsors' personal experiences with QDIAs, we developed semi-structured interview questions for a subset of survey respondents representing each QDIA type. We tailored the questions based on the responses provided to the questionnaire by each of the respondents who had provided complete contact information. We then e-mailed questions to these respondents asking them to voluntarily provide additional responses in writing or in a follow-up telephone interview. We collected written or interview responses from 28 plan sponsors using this method and analyzed the content of the responses.

Default Investment Selection

To examine which QDIA types plan sponsors use and why, we examined several quantitative and qualitative sources. To determine the number of plans that provide for automatic enrollment and use a default investment account, and the number of active participants in these plans, we examined Form 5500 data sets for the years 2009 through 2013 downloaded from the Department of Labor's website http://www.dol.gov/ebsa/foia/foia-5500.html. While the Form 5500 collects data on whether plans had a default investment for participants automatically enrolled in the plan, it does not allow plan sponsors to identify the default investment they select or whether it qualifies as a QDIA. In addition, as described above, we located and analyzed results from recurring industry surveys of plan sponsors that asked relevant questions about plans' default investment selections and corroborated these results with relevant literature and interview responses.[66]

To learn more about the attributes of each QDIA type, we collected data through our stakeholder interviews, responses to our questionnaire, and follow-up contacts with selected questionnaire respondents. In each of our stakeholder interviews, we asked which default investments plan sponsors preferred and why some sponsors might decide to select or forego QDIAs. In addition, we asked about the process sponsors used to select a specific type of QDIA, the advantages and disadvantages of each type of QDIA, and the direct and indirect factors that affected sponsors' QDIA selection process. In our questionnaire, we asked plan sponsors to comment on several aspects of QDIA selection, including the factors that most influenced their QDIA choice. We then conducted follow-up discussions with selected sponsors to obtain additional detail on why they selected their QDIAs, the role of advisors or others who provided input to their decisions, and the process they followed when making their selections. We included sponsors who selected each of the QDIA types and one sponsor who did not select a default investment.

We performed content analysis of the qualitative data to identify the primary reasons why respondents selected each type of QDIA and aspects of the selection process. In particular, we identified common themes, including the effect of plan size, sponsors' familiarity with investment vehicles, the influence of previous investment choice, and the role of third-parties such as service providers and consultants. The results of this content analysis formed the basis for our discussions in the report of the attributes for each type of QDIA and the underlying factors that influence plan sponsors' decisions.

Default Investment Monitoring

To examine how plan sponsors monitor their QDIA, we analyzed data from the same sources as we did for QDIA selection and examined selected quantitative market data on balanced fund and target-date performance. To learn more about plan sponsors' QDIA monitoring practices, we interviewed stakeholders about the frequency of sponsors' QDIA monitoring, as well as factors that might lead a sponsor to change a QDIA. In addition, we asked service providers about the performance information they provided to plan sponsors to help them monitor the QDIA and the frequency with which they provided it. In our questionnaire, we asked plans sponsors how frequently they monitored their plan's QDIA and conducted follow-up discussions with selected sponsors to obtain additional detail on their monitoring practices, including who conducted the monitoring, what performance information they used, the actions taken when warning signs appear, and the circumstances that would lead them to change a QDIA.

To better understand the types of performance information that plan sponsors use to monitor QDIAs, we reviewed relevant industry literature, analyzed sample performance reports that managed account providers sent to plan sponsors, and analyzed publicly available financial market data on balanced fund and TDF returns, risk characteristics, and cost metrics for 1-, 3-, and 5-year periods. To ensure that we examined data for funds that plan sponsors selected, we cross-referenced financial market data with select information that sponsors reported on the Form 5500 regarding the composition of a plan's investment lineup. Because the Employee Retirement Income Security Act of 1974 does not prescribe specific actions that a sponsor must take when selecting and monitoring plan investment options and, as such, two prudent plan fiduciaries with the same QDIA may look at same monitoring outcomes and arrive at different conclusions about its performance, we decided not to include quantitative illustrations of these funds' performance in the report.

Identifying Challenges

To identify challenges plan sponsors face when administering QDIAs in their 401(k)-type plans, we analyzed qualitative information from the same sources as the other objectives. As part of our interview process, we asked stakeholders to comment on sponsors' views on the sufficiency of the QDIA types, challenges plan sponsors experienced when selecting and monitoring a QDIA, and the extent to which these challenges may vary by plan size. In addition, as part of our web-based questionnaire, we asked plan sponsors to select the top three challenges they faced when selecting a specific QDIA type. Sponsors made their selections from 11 possible options or provided a narrative response. We followed up with selected questionnaire respondents to confirm their responses and solicit additional detail on why the saw these factors as challenges.

RELATED GAO REPORTS

401(k) Plans: Improvements Can Be Made to Better Protect Participants in Managed Accounts, GAO-14-310 (Washington, D.C.: June 25, 2014).

Private Pensions: Targeted Revisions Could Improve Timeliness and Content of Form 5500 Pension Information, GAO-14-441 (Washington, D.C.: June 5, 2014).

401(k) Plans: Other Countries' Experiences Offer Lessons in Policies and Oversight of Spend-down Options, GAO-14-9 (Washington, D.C.: Nov. 20, 2013).

401(k) Plans: Increased Educational Outreach and Broader Oversight May Help Reduce Plan Fees, GAO-12-325 (Washington, D.C.: April 24, 2012).

401(k) Plans: Survey of 401(k) Plan Sponsors on Fees, GAO-12-550SP (Washington, D.C.: April 2012).

Defined Contribution Plans: Key Information on Target Date Funds as Default Investments Should Be Provided to Plan Sponsors and Participants, GAO-11-118 (Washington, D.C.: Jan. 31, 2011).

Retirement Savings: Automatic Enrollment Shows Promise for Some Workers, but Proposals to Broaden Retirement Savings for Other Workers Could Face Challenges, GAO-10-31 (Washington, D.C.: Oct. 23, 2009).

End Notes

[1] Employers may sponsor DC plans and/or defined benefit (DB) plans for their employees. Under a DC plan, such as a 401(k) plan, employees have individual accounts to which the employee, employer, or both make contributions, and benefits are based on contributions, along with investment returns (gains and losses) on the accounts. See 29 U.S.C. § 1002(34) and (35). DC plans allow employees who participate in the plan to specify the size of their

contributions and direct their assets to one or more investments among the options offered within the plan.

[2] Department of Labor, Bureau of Labor Statistics, *National Compensation Survey: Employee Benefits in the United States, March 2014* Bulletin 2779 (Washington, D.C.: Sept. 2014).

[3] GAO, *Retirement Savings: Automatic Enrollment Shows Promise for Some Workers, but Proposals to Broaden Retirement Savings for Other Workers Could Face Challenges*, GAO-10-31 (Washington, D.C.: Oct. 23, 2009).

[4] Pub. L. No.109-280, § 624, 120 Stat. 780, 980 (codified as amended at 29 U.S.C. §1104(c)(5)). Specifically, the law provides in such cases that plan participants will be treated as having exercised control with respect to assets in individual account plans if such amounts are invested in a default investment in accordance with DOL regulations and participants are furnished the prescribed notice.

[5] Default Investment Alternatives Under Participant Directed Individual Account Plans, 72 Fed. Reg. 60,452 (Oct. 24, 2007) (codified at 29 C.F.R. § 2550.404c-5).

[6] Plan sponsors adopting a QDIA still need to comply with longstanding Employee Retirement Income Security Act of 1974 (ERISA) requirements that they select and monitor investment options available to plan participants, act solely in the interest of plan participants and beneficiaries in accordance with plan documents, act with prudence, and offer a diversified set of investment options with reasonable fees. 29 C.F.R. § 2550.404c-5(b)(2) and (3). Additionally, plan sponsors adopting a QDIA must notify participants prior to defaulting them into the QDIA of their ability to opt-out of the default investment, and supply them with an annual notice reminding them of this right. 29 C.F.R. § 2550.404c-5(c)(3) and (d).

[7] DOL regulations also allow plan sponsors to use capital preservation products as a short- term QDIA to afford plan sponsors the flexibility of utilizing a principal-protection investment alternative for the investment of contributions during the period of time when employees are most likely to opt out of plan participation—the first 120 days after they first make an elective contribution. 29 C.F.R. § 2550.404c-5(e)(4)(iv)(B). DOL noted that the use of capital preservation products in these circumstances will enable plan sponsors to return contributed amounts to participants who opt out without concern about loss of principal. 72 Fed. Reg. 60,463.

[8] Investment products with a mix of assets typically include (1) an equity (or stock) component, which may consist of some funds focused on equities of large U.S. corporations, international equities, or equities of smaller companies; and (2) a fixed income component, which may consist of various bond funds, such as funds comprising government and corporate bonds.

[9] Ranking Member George Miller of the House Committee on Education and the Workforce also requested that GAO conduct this work. He subsequently retired after GAO began its work.

[10] We examined data on plan default investments in the Form 5500 Annual Return/Report of Employee Benefit Plan (Form 5500)—the primary source of information for both the federal government and the private sector regarding the funding, assets, investments, and fees of pension and other employee benefit plans. We have previously reported on the Form 5500. See GAO, *Private Pensions: Targeted Revisions Could Improve Usefulness of Form 5500 Information*, GAO-14-441 (Washington, D.C.: June 5, 2014).

[11] GAO-10-31.

[12] While plans with automatic enrollment have a clear need for a default investment, other situations can occur in a 401(k) plan that may result in the need for a default investment, including incomplete enrollment forms, the removal of investment options, or assets rolled over from another plan.

[13] A record keeper maintains a recordkeeping system that is used to track contributions and returns. In some cases, the record keeper may serve as an investment manager and bundle these services for plan sponsors. These bundled services may also include an exchange of lower plan administration fees for the selection of a record keeper's investment product or service as a plan's QDIA.

[14] 29 C.F.R. § 2550.404c-5(c)(3) and (d)(1) and (2).

[15] 29 C.F.R. § 2550.404c-5(d).

[16] 29 C.F.R. § 2550.404c-5(e)(4)(i). A plan sponsor selecting a TDF as a QDIA typically selects a series of individual funds that offer different asset allocations to address different lengths of time participants have until retirement. For example, a TDF series may provide funds at 5-year intervals (e.g., 2015, 2020, and 2025 to 2060) that align with participants' estimated retirement dates. While plan sponsors typically invest QDIA contributions in the fund that corresponds with a participant's targeted retirement date, participants may choose to invest in any of the funds in the plan's investment lineup, including multiple TDF series.

[17] DOL did not distinguish between these two TDF types in its final rule.

[18] The provider of these proprietary products may be an investment management firm that also serves as the plan's record keeper.

[19] 29 C.F.R. § 2550.404c-5(e)(4)(ii).

[20] 29 C.F.R. § 2550.404c-5(e)(4)(iii).

[21] ERISA defines a plan fiduciary as anyone who (1) exercises any discretionary authority or control over plan management or the management or disposition of plan assets; (2) renders investment advice respecting plan money or other property for any compensation, or has any authority or responsibility to do so; or (3) has any discretionary authority or responsibility for plan administration. 29 U.S.C. § 1002(21). DOL recently published a proposed rule that would treat persons who provide investment advice or recommendations to an employee benefit plan, plan fiduciary, plan participant or beneficiary, individual retirement account (IRA), or IRA owner as plan fiduciaries; ensure that such investment advice is in the best interest of their clients; and allow clients to hold those who provide investment advice to them accountable. Definition of the Term ''Fiduciary''; Conflict of Interest Rule—Retirement Investment Advice, 80 Fed. Reg. 21,928 (Apr. 20, 2015).

[22] 29 U.S.C. § 1104(a).

[23] 72 Fed. Reg. 60,453. DOL guidance suggests that plan sponsors document decisions and the basis for those decisions. For example, a fiduciary may want to survey a number of potential providers, asking for the same information and specifying the same requirements. Such methods allow a plan sponsor to make a meaningful comparison and selection. See DOL, EBSA, *Meeting Your Fiduciary Responsibilities* (Government Printing Office: Washington, D.C.: Feb. 2012).

[24] 29 C.F.R. § 2550.404c-5(b)(2).

[25] Plan service providers that have investment discretion or provide investment advice about how to invest participant accounts are generally referred to as either "3(38) Investment Manager" fiduciaries or "3(21) Investment Adviser" fiduciaries, depending on their role in the plan. GAO-14-310. Under section 3(38) of ERISA, "3(38) Investment Manager" fiduciaries have the power to manage, acquire, or dispose of plan assets, and they acknowledge, in writing, that they are a fiduciary with respect to the plan. 29 U.S.C. § 1002(38). In contrast, under section 3(21) of ERISA, 3(21) Investment Adviser fiduciaries usually do not have authority to manage, acquire, or dispose of plan assets, but they are still fiduciaries because their investment recommendations may exercise some level of influence and control over the investments made by a plan. 29 U.S.C. § 1002(21). When managed account services are

offered as QDIAs, the managed account provider is generally required to be a 3(38) Investment Manager fiduciary. 29 C.F.R. § 2550.404c-5(e)(4)(iii) and (e)(3)(i).

[26] Title I of ERISA applies to private-sector pension plans (29 U.S.C. § 1003(b)); EBSA is not responsible for enforcement pertaining to public-sector plans.

[27] DOL collects limited data on plans' use of default investments from plans required to file the Form 5500. Since 2009, DC plans have been required to indicate on their annual Form 5500 filings whether (1) a plan "provides for automatic enrollment in a plan that has elective contributions deducted from payroll," and (2) if, in case of participant directed account plans, a plan "uses default investment account for participants who fail to direct assets in their account." Sponsors do not have to identify the default investment they use or whether it is a QDIA.

[28] We reviewed the results of several annual industry surveys of plan sponsors, selecting three that reported consistent annual data on sponsors' use of default investments for the most consecutive years since DOL issued final QDIA regulations (i.e., 2009-2013). PLANSPONSOR (Survey A), the Callan Investments Institute (Survey B), and Deloitte (Survey C) conducted the annual surveys that we reviewed. In 2013, the surveys collected 5,342; 107; and 265 responses, respectively. For more information on the surveys, including the industries and the amount of plan assets that each survey represented, see appendix I.

[29] We use the general term "stakeholders" in this report to refer to a wide range of individuals knowledgeable of different aspects of 401(k) plans, participants, and investments. We obtained stakeholder views directly through semi-structured interviews and indirectly through content analysis of the literature on QDIAs in 401(k) plans. The views presented here may not incorporate all stakeholder viewpoints. References to plan sponsors' views are based on responses obtained from plan sponsors who responded to our questionnaire. Similarly, these views are not generalizable and may not incorporate all plan sponsor views.

[30] Plan sponsors responding to the questionnaire may have included more than one reason why they selected a particular type of QDIA.

[31] For example, sponsors with a custom TDF can design a glide path that incorporates the interaction among multiple factors, such as other retirement benefits or assets, contribution and payout patterns, and inflation. These sponsors can also have greater control over plan design, fees, and asset managers, and can address known risks that are specific to the organization or employees. Used primarily by large plans, custom TDFs can be cost-effective because sponsors can reduce fees by placing more assets with fewer managers.

[32] We did not undertake a compliance assessment to determine the extent to which plan fiduciaries included in our study had exercised due diligence in selecting, monitoring, or comparing various QDIAs because this was outside the scope of our work.

[33] A plan merger may change the overall participant demographic profile of a plan, leading a plan sponsor to have to consider whether the current QDIA is still appropriate for the participant population or a change is required.

[34] According to DOL officials, the frequency of monitoring depends on a plan's facts and circumstances. Sponsors and stakeholders stated that QDIA monitoring is typically conducted as part of a plan's review of its investment lineup.

[35] 29 C.F.R. § 25.404c-5(e)(4)(i) and (iii).

[36] 29 C.F.R. § 25.404c-5(e)(4)(ii).

[37] 72 Fed. Reg. 60,461.

[38] Other plan sponsors stated that their plans' investment committees retained sufficient discretion to take current circumstances into account when making decisions on their investments so

that they are not compelled to take actions that may not be in the best interest of participants.

[39] Index funds are generally passively managed funds that seek to track the performance of a market index, such as the S&P 500. In contrast, actively managed funds have specific investment goals (e.g., outperforming a market index or peer groups) and strategies that inform investment managers' research and selection of investments.

[40] Some stakeholders said that in contrast to custom TDFs, off-the-shelf TDFs were more likely to use funds not part of a plans' existing investment lineup, making it necessary for sponsors to perform an additional step in their due diligence review of the underlying funds. However, other stakeholders indicated that because most off-the-shelf TDFs were publicly traded funds, sponsors who selected them as QDIAs could benefit from available performance information and third-party analysis that may not be available for custom TDFs.

[41] We previously reported that more consistent performance information from managed account providers would allow plan sponsors to more effectively make comparisons in their selection and monitoring. GAO-14-310.

[42] Stakeholders spoke of general trends and behavior among "large" and "small" plans in the overall plan sponsor industry and noted that resources and expertise vary among similarly-sized plans. They said that there are small plans that are as sophisticated as many of their larger counterparts but that these instances were more exceptions than the norm. For more information on recent trends in 401(k) plans, see GAO, *401(k) Plans: Survey of 401(k) Plan Sponsors on Fees*, GAO-12-550SP (Washington, D.C.: April 2012).

[43] Some stakeholders stated that the resource and expertise discrepancy between large and small plan sponsors partly explains why large plan sponsors are more likely than small plans to use TDFs, especially custom solutions. For example, TDFs are more complicated to monitor, and larger plans—which typically have the resources and expertise to monitor them—are more likely to select them. However, some stakeholders stated that many plan sponsors—especially smaller plan sponsors—may choose a QDIA simply because they observe or perceive other plans doing the same, without consideration for the resources or expertise that may be required to monitor it.

[44] Exec. Order No. 12866, 58 Fed. Reg. 51,735 (Sept. 30, 1993).

[45] 29 C.F.R. § 2550.404c-5(e)(4)(i) and (iii).

[46] 29 C.F.R. § 2550.404c-5(e)(4)(ii).

[47] 72 Fed. Reg. 60,461.

[48] GAO, *Defined Contribution Plans: Key Information on Target Date Funds as Default Investments Should Be Provided to Plan Sponsors and Participants*, GAO-11-118 (Washington, D.C: Jan. 31, 2011).

[49] DOL/EBSA, *Target Date Retirement Funds—Tips for ERISA Plan Fiduciaries*. (Washington, D.C.: Feb. 2013).

[50] 29 C.F.R. § 2550.404c-5(e)(4)(ii).

[51] 72 Fed. Reg. 60,477.

[52] 72 Fed. Reg. 60,453. According to DOL officials, a plan fiduciary may, at its discretion, select any of the eligible investment products to be a QDIA, and the choice among the three options is itself not a separate fiduciary decision. DOL does not require that plan fiduciaries separately, and without the benefit of the fiduciary relief provided by the rule, make their own determination whether one of the categories is more appropriate than the others.

[53] Some sponsors found DOL's 2013 tip sheet on TDF selection to be helpful. Among other things, it encouraged plan sponsors to inquire whether off-the-shelf or custom TDFs would

be a better fit for their plans. One stakeholder told us that sponsors may interpret this guidance as endorsing custom TDFs as a better QDIA solution. DOL officials stated that while customized investment products may offer advantages, a plan fiduciary must weigh the possible advantages of using a customized investment product against potential costs and administrative burdens involved in creating and maintaining such a product. Sponsors also noted that they would welcome similar guidance on the other QDIA types. See DOL/EBSA, *Target Date Retirement Funds—Tips for ERISA Plan Fiduciaries.*

[54] Re-enrollment can involve enrolling employees who previously elected not to participate in or left a plan, switching participants enrolled in one plan into another plan, and changing a participant's investment allocations within a plan. Sponsors are required to notify participants of their right to make an election at least 30 days prior to any first investment in a QDIA being made on their behalf. 29 C.F.R. § 2550.404c-5(c)(3)(i)(A). In addition, they must send an annual notice to affected participants reminding them of their right to direct the investments in their accounts. 29 C.F.R. § 2550.404c-5(c)(3)(ii).

[55] Funds that experience sustained poor performance, a failure to gather assets, or a combination of performance and operational failure are often closed by the provider. Vanguard recently reported that from 1997 through 2011, more than 2,000 mutual funds had either been merged with other funds or been liquidated.

[56] In prior work, we recommended that DOL expand the investment alternatives available for forced-transfer IRAs to include additional investments, such as ones that qualify as QDIAs to prevent forced-transfer IRA balances from decreasing due to the low returns of the safe-harbor investment options. DOL disagreed with our recommendation saying that Congress intended these assets to be invested in a way that preserved the principal transferred out of plans. However, our analysis showed that many forced-transfer IRAs have experienced very large and even complete declines in principal. We continue to believe that our recommendation should be implemented and encourage DOL to expand the safe harbor under 29 C.F.R. § 2550.404a-2 to include investment alternatives more likely to preserve principal and even increase it over time. See GAO, *401(k) Plans: Greater Protections Needed for Forced Transfers and Inactive Accounts* GAO-15-73 (Washington, D.C.: Nov. 21, 2014).

[57] *Bidwell v. Univ. Med. Ctr. Inc.*, 685 F.3d 613 (6th Cir. 2012). The trial and appellate courts both ruled in favor of the plan sponsor. The appellate court noted that the preamble to the final QDIA regulations emphasized that whenever a participant has the opportunity to direct the investment of account assets but does not, plan fiduciaries may receive fiduciary relief under the regulations so long as all the other safe harbor requirements in the regulations are met.

[58] Annuities are guaranteed payments that are normally secured through a contract with an insurance company for either a set period or for the participant's lifetime. Annuities come in a variety of forms. For example, deferred annuities allow participants to delay the start date of payments to a later point in retirement. Variable annuity payments are not guaranteed and vary based on the performance of underlying investments selected by the participant. For more information on annuities and other spend-down options in the United States and other countries, see GAO, *401(k) Plans: Other Countries' Experiences Offer Lessons in Policies and Oversight of Spend-down Options*, GAO-14-9 (Washington, D.C.: Nov. 20, 2013).

[59] In a letter to the Department of the Treasury, DOL addressed the application of the QDIA regulations and annuity selection safe harbor (29 C.F.R. § 2550.404a-4) to a series of TDFs that included unallocated deferred annuity contracts as part of the funds' "fixed income" component. The letter concluded that the use of these types of TDFs met the requirements

of the QDIA regulations. DOL, *Letter to the Department of Treasury's Senior Advisor to the Secretary and Deputy Assistant Secretary for Retirement and Health Policy*, dated Oct. 23, 2014.

[60] 29 C.F.R. § 2550.404c-5(a)(2).

[61] As we previously reported, some TDFs experienced large losses in the 2008 recession due to high concentrations in equities. See GAO-11-118. In our review of recent data from TDF series offered by three large service providers—Vanguard, Fidelity, and T. Rowe Price—we found equity allocations in TDFs with a 2015 target retirement date ranging from 44 to 57 percent.

[62] According to DOL's Field Assistance Bulletin 2008-03 (issued April 29, 2008), its QDIA regulations do not preclude a plan fiduciary from selecting more than one of the eligible QDIAs. DOL officials noted that the QDIA regulations would allow a plan to continue to use a balanced fund from one plan and the managed account from another plan following a corporate merger.

[63] Asset International, *2014 Plan Benchmarking Report: Overall Results from the 2013 Plansponsor Defined Contribution Survey*, Downloadable for a fee from http://www.assetinternational.com/research-library.aspx.

[64] Callan Investments Institute, 2014 Defined Contribution Trends. Downloadable for a fee from https://www.callan.com/research/DC/.

[65] Deloitte, *Annual Defined Contribution Benchmarking Survey*. Downloadable at no cost from http://www2.deloitte.com/us/en/pages/human-capital/articles/annual-defined-contribution-benchmarking-survey.html.

[66] We did not undertake a compliance assessment to determine the extent to which plan fiduciaries included in our study had exercised due diligence in selecting, monitoring, or comparing various QDIAs because this was outside the scope of our work.

In: 401(k) Plans
Editor: Wesley Meyer

ISBN: 978-1-63484-727-8

Chapter 2

RETIREMENT SAVINGS: AUTOMATIC ENROLLMENT SHOWS PROMISE FOR SOME WORKERS, BUT PROPOSALS TO BROADEN RETIREMENT SAVINGS FOR OTHER WORKERS COULD FACE CHALLENGES*

United States Government Accountability Office

WHY GAO DID THIS STUDY

Although employer-sponsored retirement plans can be an important component of income security after retirement, only about half of all workers participate in such plans. To foster greater participation among workers who have access to such plans, Congress included provisions that facilitate plan sponsors' adoption of automatic enrollment policies in the Pension Protection Act of 2006. To foster greater retirement savings among workers who do not have access to an employer-sponsored plan, proposals have been made at the federal level for an "automatic IRA" and at the state level for state- based programs.

Because of questions about the extent of retirement savings and prospects for a sound retirement for all Americans, GAO was asked to determine (1)

* This is an edited, reformatted and augmented version of a report, GAO-10-31, issued by the United States Government Accountability Office, October 2009.

what is known about the effect of automatic enrollment policies among the nation's 401(k) plans, and the extent of and future prospect for such policies; and (2) the potential benefits and limitations of automatic IRA proposals and state-assisted retirement savings proposals. To answer these questions, GAO reviewed available reports and data, and interviewed plan sponsors, industry groups, investment professionals, and relevant federal agencies.

WHAT GAO RECOMMENDS

This report makes no recommendations.

WHAT GAO FOUND

Automatic enrollment appears to significantly increase participation in 401(k) plans according to existing studies, but may not be suitable for all plan sponsors. Some studies found that participation rates can reach as high as 95 percent under automatic enrollment. Available data indicate that the percentage of plans with automatic enrollment policies increased from about 1 percent in 2004 to more than 16 percent in 2009, with higher rates of adoption among larger plan sponsors. In most cases, these plans automatically enroll only new employees, rather than all employees. We also found that automatic enrollment may not be suitable for all plan sponsors, such as those with a high-turnover workforce. Further, some data show that while automatic escalation policies—which automatically increase saving rates over time—are increasingly common, they lag behind adoption of automatic enrollment. In combination with low initial contribution rates, this could depress savings for some workers. Also, the emergence of target-date funds—funds that allocate investments among various asset classes and shift to lower-risk investments as a "target" retirement date approaches—as the typical default investment raises questions in light of the substantial losses such funds experienced in the past year.

Other proposals could expand the portion of the workforce saving for retirement, but these proposals could face challenges. Under a federally mandated automatic IRA, certain employers could be required to enroll eligible employees in payroll-deduction IRAs, unless the worker specifically opted out. Such a proposal could broaden the population that saves for retirement at minimal cost to employers. However, this proposal faces a number of challenges, including uncertainty about the extent to which it would help low-income workers accumulate significant retirement savings. Proposals for state-assisted retirement savings programs could raise coverage and, ultimately, savings by involving state governments in facilitating retirement savings for workers without access to an employer-sponsored plan. However, such programs face uncertainty about employer and worker participation levels, as well as legal and regulatory issues.

ABBREVIATIONS

ABC	American Benefits Council
ASPPA	American Society of Pension Professionals and Actuaries
CAP	Center for American Progress
CIEBA	The Committee on Investment of Employee Benefit Assets
EBRI	Employee Benefits Research Institute
ERISA	Employee Retirement Income Security Act of 1974
ICI	Investment Company Institute
IRA	individual retirement account
IRS	Internal Revenue Service
PPA	Pension Protection Act of 2006
PRC	Pension Rights Center
PSCA	Profit Sharing/401(k) Council of America
QDIA	Qualified Default Investment Alternative
SBCA	Small Business Council of America
SIMPLE	Savings Incentive Match Plan for Employees of Small Employers
SIPP	Survey of Income and Program Participation
TDF	target-date fund

* * *

October 23, 2009
The Honorable Herb Kohl
Chairman
Special Committee on Aging
United States Senate

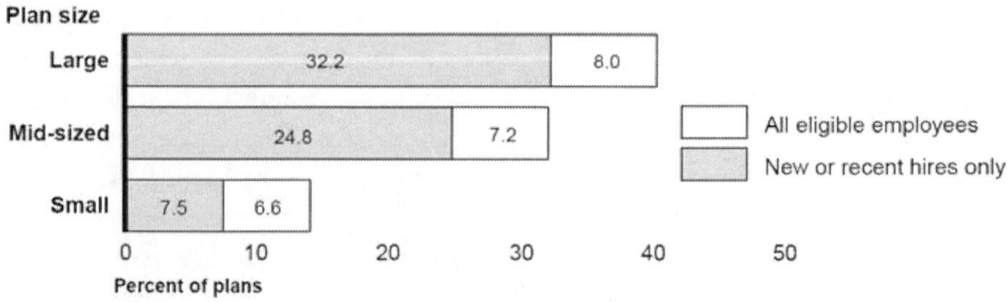

Source: GAO presentation of Fidelity Investments data.

Adoption and Scope of Automatic Enrollment by Plan Size, March 2009.

Dear Mr. Chairman:

Although employer-sponsored retirement plans can be an important component of retirement security for millions of American workers, only about half of all workers participate in such plans. Further, there has been little change in the percentage of workers covered by employer-sponsored plans in the last quarter century. While some working Americans choose not to participate in an employer-sponsored retirement savings plan, the large majority of uncovered workers do not have access to an employer- sponsored plan. Non-participation in employer-sponsored plans may have significant implications for future income, particularly for low-income workers. For example, as GAO reported in 2007, about 63 percent of workers in the lowest income quartile are projected to have no defined contribution plan savings at retirement.[1] Further, workers in this quartile are projected to have savings that would replace an average of about 10.3 percent of their annualized career earnings after retirement, compared to replacement rates of about 34 percent for the highest income quartile.

To foster retirement saving among the portion of the workforce that has been offered an employer-sponsored retirement savings plan but does not participate in it, some employers have adopted automatic enrollment policies for their defined contribution plans—retirement plans under which participants accumulate retirement savings in individual accounts, such as a 401(k). Under automatic enrollment, a worker is enrolled into the plan automatically, or by default, unless they explicitly choose to opt out. Employers who have adopted automatic enrollment must also establish default contribution rates and default investment vehicles for workers who do not specify these choices on their own. Employers may also adopt automatic escalation policies, which increase contribution rates automatically over time—typically up to a pre-defined maximum contribution rate per participant.

In addition, federal and state legislators have introduced proposals to foster retirement savings among those who work for employers that do not sponsor a plan. One group of proposals calls for establishing automatic individual retirement accounts (IRA) for workers not covered by another retirement plan. Under an automatic IRA, employers would be required to offer their employees the opportunity to make contributions through automatic payroll deduction, with an opt-out provision for participants. Another set of proposals calls for state governments to facilitate the establishment of retirement accounts for private-sector workers who are not covered by employer-sponsored plans. However, as of July 2009, no proposals for a federal automatic IRA or a state-assisted retirement savings plan had been passed into law.

In light of your interest in increasing retirement savings and ensuring a sound retirement for all Americans, you asked us to examine certain options for expanding retirement plan coverage. Specifically, we addressed the following two questions:

1. What is known about the effect of automatic enrollment policies among the nation's 401(k) plans, as well as the extent of and prospects for such policies?
2. What are the potential benefits and limitations of automatic IRA proposals and state-assisted retirement savings proposals?

To answer the first question, we obtained and reviewed data collected by large 401(k) plan administrators; reviewed studies on the impact of 401(k) automatic enrollment polices on participation rates and saving patterns; and conducted in-depth interviews with selected plan sponsors about their experience with and views of automatic enrollment. We found the data from these sources to be sufficiently reliable for our use. To answer the second question, we reviewed and analyzed existing proposals, as well as feasibility studies of these proposals, and interviewed pension industry experts in academia, representatives of employee benefit consulting firms, plan administrators, and state and federal government officials. Throughout this report, we considered a worker to be covered by an employer-sponsored plan if the employer offers such a plan, the worker is eligible to participate under the plan's rules, and the worker chooses to participate in it. For both objectives, we also reviewed relevant federal regulations.

We conducted this audit from August 2008 to October 2009 in accordance with generally accepted government auditing standards. Those standards require that we plan and perform the audit to obtain sufficient, appropriate evidence to provide a reasonable basis for our findings and conclusions based on our audit objectives. We believe that the evidence obtained provides a reasonable basis for our findings and conclusions based on our audit objectives. Appendix I of this report contains a detailed description of the methodology used in this review and its limitations.

BACKGROUND

Traditionally, employers that sponsored retirement plans generally established "defined benefit" plans. Under such plans, participation is generally automatic for eligible workers, and retirement benefits are established by a formula, often based on a worker's salary and years of service. Since the 1980s, defined contribution plans—most prominently the 401(k) plan—have supplanted defined benefit plans as the dominant type of private-sector retirement plan. Under defined contribution plans, workers typically must decide whether or not to participate, how much to contribute, and how to invest plan assets from a range of options provided under the plan. Under a 401(k) plan, if the employee does not participate, if contributions made to an employee's account are insufficient, or if the investments that an employee chooses yield an inadequate return, the employee may have retirement income that is insufficient to maintain his or her desired standard of living.

As defined contribution plans emerged as the dominant form of retirement plan, the percentage of the population covered by employer-sponsored plans changed very little—remaining at about half of the workforce. As figure 1 shows, Current Population Survey data reveal that about 48 percent of the total U.S. workforce was not covered by an employer- sponsored a plan in 2007.[2] About 40 percent worked for an employer that did not sponsor a plan, and about 8 percent did not participate in the plan that their employer sponsored.

According to the Current Population Survey, certain segments of the working population have consistently had much lower rates of employment with employers sponsoring a plan, and lower participation rates than the working population overall. As figure 2 illustrates, larger portions of certain worker groups, such as lower-income workers, younger workers, workers employed by smaller companies, and part-time workers lack coverage compared to all full-time workers.

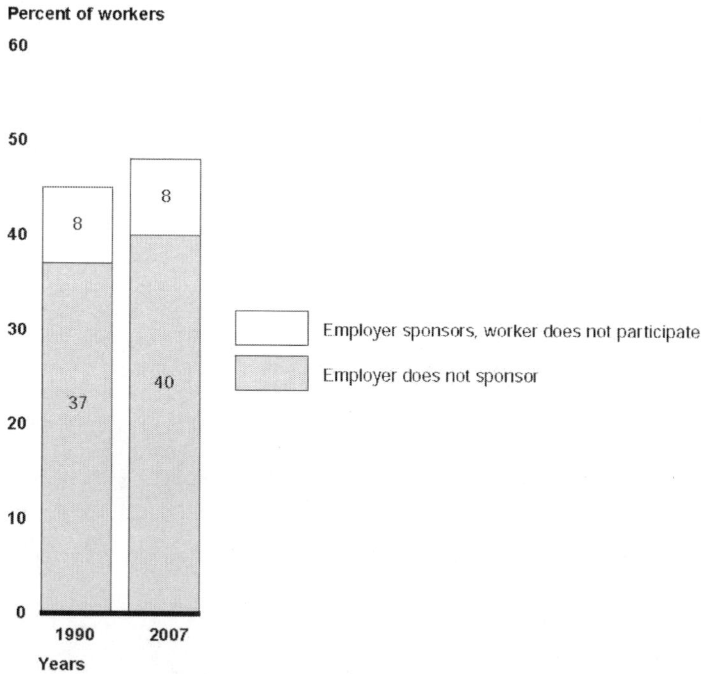

Source: GAO presentation of data in Pension Sponsorship and Participation: Summary of Recent Trends, Congressional Research Service, September 2008.

Figure 1. Proportion of Full-Time Workforce Lacking Retirement Plan Coverage, 1990 and 2007.

Workers may choose not to enroll, or delay enrolling, in a retirement plan for a number of reasons. For example, according to a recent Congressional Research Service presentation of data from the Survey of Income and Program Participation, most non-participating workers whose employer sponsored a plan said they thought—in some cases, incorrectly—they were ineligible.[3] The report also found that substantial numbers of employees fail to participate because they believe they cannot afford to contribute to the plan. For example, 19 percent of nonparticipating respondents cited this reason, and 10 percent said they did not want to tie up their money. In recent years, exponents of "behavioral economics" have noted that many non-participants may not have made a specific decision, but rather fail to participate because of a tendency to procrastinate and follow the path that does not require an active decision. Further, some workers may not participate because of more immediate savings objectives—such as saving for education or a home—and, in the case of lower income workers, the prospect that Social Security benefits will replace a relatively high percentage of income in their retirement years. For example, a recent analysis by the Investment Company Institute concluded that lower income workers are less likely to save for retirement in part because Social Security benefits replace a higher proportion of their pre-retirement earnings.[4]

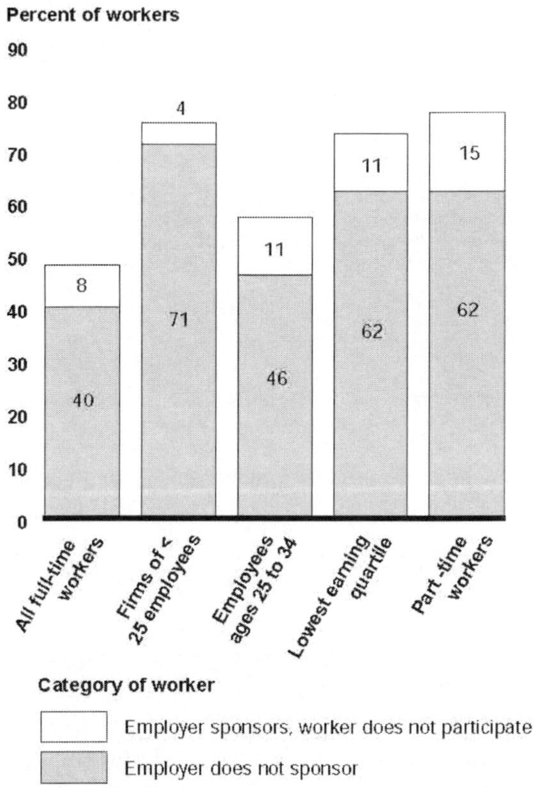

Source: GAO presentation of data in Pension Sponsorship and Participation: Summary of Recent Trends, Congressional Research Service, September 2008.
Note: Except where noted, all data are for full-time workers only.

Figure 2. Proportion of Labor Force That Lacked Retirement Plan Coverage in 2007, by Selected Worker Characteristics.

In recent years, automatic enrollment has been advocated as a way to encourage greater participation in 401(k) plans among the portion of the workforce who have access to such plans but opt not to participate. Typically, under 401(k)s and some other types of defined contribution plans, workers have been required to decide whether or not to join a plan, to specify their saving contribution rates, and to select investments from the range of investment options offered by the plan.[5] Under automatic enrollment, in contrast, a worker would be enrolled in a plan unless she or he explicitly opted-out of the plan. Plan sponsors that adopt automatic enrollment must specify a default contribution rate—the portion of an employee's salary that will be deposited in the plan—that applies to employees who do not choose a different contribution rate. Also, plan sponsors must select a default investment—the fund or other vehicle into which deferred savings will be invested—unless the employee specifies an investment or investments from those available under the plan. Employers may also adopt an automatic escalation policy, under which an employee's contribution rates would be automatically increased at periodic intervals, such as annually. For example, if the default contribution rate is 3 percent of pay, a plan sponsor may choose to increase an employee's rate of saving by 1 percent per year, up to some maximum, such as 6 percent. While a plan sponsor that adopts an automatic enrollment policy must specify a default contribution rate and a default investment, plan features such as these and automatic escalation may also be adopted in the absence of an automatic enrollment policy.

Automatic enrollment has not been a traditional feature of 401(k) plans and, prior to 1998, plan sponsors feared that adopting automatic enrollment could lead to plan disqualification.[6] However, in 1998, the Internal Revenue Service (IRS) addressed this issue by stating that a plan sponsor could automatically enroll newly hired employees and, in 2000, clarified that automatic enrollment is permissible for current employees who have not enrolled.[7] Nonetheless, a number of considerations inhibited widespread adoption of automatic enrollment, including remaining concerns such as liability in the event that the employee's investments under the plan did not perform satisfactorily, and concerns about state laws that prohibit withholding employee pay without written employee consent. More recently, provisions of the Pension Protection Act of 2006 (PPA) and subsequent regulations further facilitated the adoption of automatic enrollment by providing incentives for doing so and by protecting plans from fiduciary and legal liability if certain conditions are met.[8] In September 2009, the Department of the Treasury announced IRS actions designed to further promote automatic enrollment and the use of automatic escalation policies.[9]

Other proposals have been put forth with the intent of broadening the practice of saving for retirement among workers whose employers do not sponsor a retirement plan. One such proposal is the automatic IRA, which would require employers that do not sponsor a retirement plan to facilitate direct deposit or payroll-deduction savings for all employees.[10] To maximize participation, employees would be automatically enrolled, but would be permitted to opt out. Legislative proposals to establish an automatic IRA requirement were introduced in Congress in 2006 and 2007, and the concept of an automatic IRA was also mentioned in the President's 2010 Budget proposal.[11] In addition, legislative proposals have been introduced in some states' legislatures that would involve state governments in facilitating payroll-deduction retirement plans or IRAs for employers that do not already offer them.[12] According to the architect of the state plan concept, a state could play an intermediary role to pool assets and share expenses among many plan sponsors, thus lowering costs.

PPA Provisions Facilitating Automatic Enrollment

Anti-Discrimination Safe Harbor 401(k) (13)

Plans that adopt automatic enrollment may be exempt from required annual testing to ensure that the plan does not discriminate in favor of highly compensated employees. To obtain safe harbor protection, plans must adopt automatic enrollment as well as other plan features and policies. For example, the plan must:

- Notify affected employees about automatic contributions
- Defer at least 3 percent of pay in the first year
- Automatically increase contribution by 1 percent each subsequent year, to a minimum of 6 percent and a maximum of 10 percent
- Invest savings in a type of investment vehicle identified in Department of Labor regulations as a Qualified Default Investment Alternative (QDIA)[a]

- Match 100 percent of the first 1 percent of employee contributions, and 50 percent of contributions beyond 1 percent, up to 6 percent of wages

Protection from Employee Retirement Income Security Act of 1974 (ERISA) Fiduciary Liability

In the absence of direction from an employee, plans that automatically invest contributions in a QDIA are treated as if the employee exercised control over management of their savings in the plan. As a result, plans that comply with Department of Labor regulations pertaining to QDIAs will not be liable for any loss that occurs as a result of such investments.

90-Day Withdrawal Period

An automatically enrolled worker has 90 days to opt out and withdraw any contributions (including the earnings on those contributions.) These amounts will not be subject to the extra tax that normally applies to distributions received before age 59½. 414(w)(2)(B).

Protection from State Wage-Garnishment Laws

PPA preempts any state law that would directly or indirectly prohibit or restrict the inclusion of an automatic enrollment arrangement in a plan.

Source: GAO analysis of Pension Protection Act and related regulations.

[a] Final regulations issued by the U.S. Department of Labor specify four categories of QDIAs. They are (1) a product with a mix of investments that takes into account an individual's age (such as a target- date fund), (2) an investment service that allocates assets according to an individual's age (such as a managed account), or (3) a product with a mix of investments that takes into account the characteristics of the group of employees as a whole, rather than each individual (such as a balanced fund). A sponsor may also use a capital preservation fund as a QDIA for the first 120 days of an individual's participation to simplify administration if the worker opts out of the plan. 29 C.F.R. §2550.404c-5(c)(4).

AUTOMATIC ENROLLMENT RAISES PLAN PARTICIPATION, BUT SOME PLAN SPONSORS HAVE NOT ADOPTED PLAN FEATURES THAT COULD FURTHER FACILITATE RETIREMENT SAVINGS

Existing studies show that automatic enrollment significantly increases participation rates in 401(k) plans, although beneficial effects of automatic enrollment may depend on accompanying policies designed to ensure adequate savings and appropriate investment. While defined contribution plan sponsors have increasingly adopted automatic enrollment in recent years, this approach may not be suitable for all plan sponsors, and available data show that some plan sponsors have not augmented automatic enrollment policies with other policies designed to ensure adequate savings.

Automatic Enrollment Increases Participation Rates, but Some Participants' Acceptance of the Default Contribution Rate and Investment Fund May Limit Savings Potential

According to analyses we reviewed, automatic enrollment policies result in considerably increased 401(k) participation rates for plans adopting them, with some participation rates reaching as high as 95 percent.[13] For example, one study followed comparison groups hired before and after a company adopted automatic enrollment for new employees only and compared the participation rates of the two groups. The participation rate for those hired before automatic enrollment was adopted was 37 percent at 3 to 15 months of tenure, compared with an 86 percent participation rate for the group hired after automatic enrollment with a similar amount of tenure.[14] According to the studies we reviewed, automatic enrollment has this effect because many people find it easier to delay the decision to enroll in a plan out of inertia, procrastination, feelings of intimidation about making savings and investment decisions, or other factors. Workers may intellectually understand the importance of saving for retirement but have trouble overcoming their own inertia to start saving or to save effectively.[15] A team of researchers found that under automatic enrollment, workers' inertia works in favor of saving for retirement because workers need to do little or nothing to participate in their employers' plan.[16] Further, workers may also decline to participate, in part, because they believe the decision to participate in a 401(k) plan requires time-consuming and complex decisions, such as choosing how much to contribute and how to invest their contributions. Automatic enrollment, through its default contribution rates and default investment vehicles, offers an easier way to start saving.[17] Table 1 shows overall participation rate increases reported in the various studies we reviewed.

Table 1. Overall Participation Rate Effects of Automatic Enrollment

Study	Authors (year of study)	Overall participation rate	
		Percent under voluntary enrollment only	Percent under automatic enrollment
The Power of Suggestion[a]	Madrian and Shea (2001)	37	86
For Better or For Worse[a]	Choi et al. (2001)	26-43[b]	85 and above
Nationwide Savings Plan Automatic Enrollment Getting Associates PREPared for Retirement[a]	Swanson and Farnen (2008)	77	95
The Importance of Default Options for Retirement Saving Outcomes: Evidence from the United States[a]	Beshears et al. (2008)	60	95
Building Futures Volume VIII	Fidelity Investments (2007)	53	81
Measuring the Effectiveness of Automatic Enrollment	Vanguard Center for Retirement Research (2007)	45	86

Source: GAO analysis.

[a] These studies are based on a small number of case studies.

[b] After 6 months of tenure. This study reports separate results for three case-study companies.

Three of the studies also found that automatic enrollment has a significant effect on subgroups of workers with relatively low participation rates, such as lower-income and younger workers. For example, the Fidelity Investments study found that 30 percent of workers aged 20 to 29 were participating in plans without automatic enrollment. In plans with automatic enrollment, the participation rate for workers in that age range was 77 percent, an increase of 47 percentage points.[18] In addition, four of the studies found that automatic enrollment policies reduced the disparities in participation rates between certain groups of workers. For example, the Madrian and Shea study examined participation rates by race and ethnicity and found that, among workers hired under a voluntary enrollment only policy, Hispanic workers had the lowest participation rate at 19.0 percent, blacks had a slightly higher participation rate of 21.7 percent, and whites had the highest participation rate at 42.7 percent. Under automatic enrollment, however, the participation rates for Hispanic and black employees nearly quadrupled to 75.1 percent and 81.3 percent, respectively, narrowing the gap with white workers, whose participation rate more than doubled, increasing to 88.2 percent. The difference in participation rates between white and Hispanic employees fell from 23.7 to 13.1 percentage points.[19]

The high level of participation rates under automatic enrollment appears to persist after such policies are adopted, according to two of the studies in our review.[20] Both studies observed participation rates at specific companies for about 3 years after an automatic enrollment policy was adopted. The studies found that for employees hired under automatic enrollment, participation jumped almost immediately and then increased slightly over the 3-year period, but remained relatively stable. The Vanguard study modeled the participation rate over time and found a decline in the participation rate over a 3-year period, with the participation rate falling by about 10 percentage points from its peak of 91 percent but remaining high relative to participation rates for plans without automatic enrollment.[21] Consistent with these results, plan sponsors who had adopted automatic enrollment stated that their experience also indicated that higher participation rates were sustained. One plan sponsor, a large manufacturer, reported that after 2 years of automatic enrollment, 95 percent of employees who had been automatically enrolled had stayed in the plan.[22]

Although automatic enrollment can increase participation and saving rates for most workers, it may have an adverse effect on saving rates and investment choices for other workers, depending on the nature of default contribution rates and default investment funds used, according to some of the studies in our review. Four of the six studies we reviewed found that automatically enrolled participants are likely to accept the plan's default contribution rate. Three of the studies found that some participants would have selected a contribution rate higher than the default rate had they not been subject to automatic enrollment and had they chosen to enroll in the plan voluntarily. Further, two of the three studies also found that some participants were likely to accept a default investment fund with relatively low future prospects for return on investment, such as money-market or stable-value funds, compared to the investment fund they would have selected if they had voluntary enrolled.[23] Thus, these studies concluded that overall savings for these particular participants were lower under automatic enrollment.[24] Further, the Beshears et al. study calculated participation rates for a company that doubled its default contribution rate from 3 percent to 6 percent and found that the participation rates were virtually identical before and after the policy change. In addition, Fidelity Investments reported that employees accept the default contribution rate the majority of the time, regardless of how high it is. Studies have found that default policies have these effects, in part, for the same reasons that automatic enrollment increases participation rates—accepting the defaults is the path of least resistance and requires no action on the part of the worker. In addition, some studies found that some employees see default policies as implicit advice from the plan sponsor and that they imply optimal saving rates and investment choices.

Adoption of Automatic Enrollment Has Grown Considerably in Recent Years, but Many Plan Sponsors Have Not Adopted Policies to Ensure Adequate Long-Term Savings

Automatic enrollment policies have been increasingly adopted by defined contribution plan sponsors in recent years as a result of several factors. Nonetheless, a number of considerations may limit adoption of automatic enrollment over the long term. Low default contribution rates and an apparent lag in the adoption of automatic escalation policies raise questions about the adequacy of long-term saving rates under automatic enrollment. Further, the widespread adoption of target-date funds (TDF)—funds that allocate investments among various asset classes and automatically shift to lower-risk, income-producing investments as a "target" retirement date approaches—as default investments for plans with automatic enrollment has raised concerns about investment risk and transparency of investments of TDFs for participants nearing retirement.

Greater Adoption of Automatic Enrollment and Factors Driving Trend

Data from two large plan administrators, as well as discussion with retirement plan experts, indicate that plan sponsors' adoption of such policies has grown considerably in recent years. Data from Fidelity Investments show that the percentage of defined contribution plans adopting automatic enrollment grew from about 1 percent in December 2004 to about 16 percent in March of 2009. Comparable data from Vanguard show that about 19 percent of plans had adopted automatic enrollment as of December 2008, up from 8 percent in June 2006.

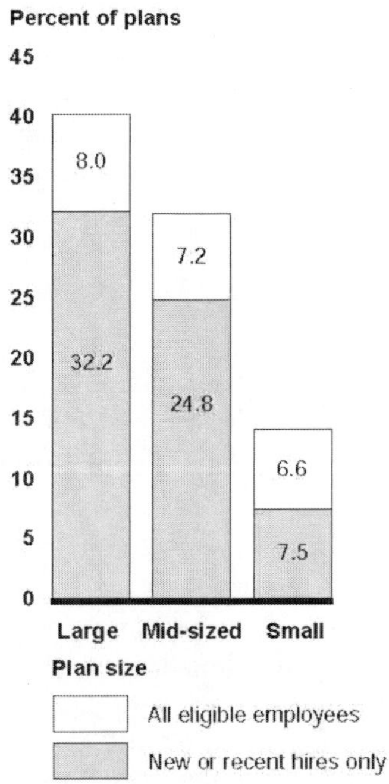

Source: GAO presentation of Fidelity Investments data.

Figure 3. Adoption and Scope of Automatic Enrollment by Plan Size, March 2009.

Data from one plan administrator show that large plan sponsors—sponsors of plans with $500 million or more in assets—have adopted automatic enrollment policies more often than smaller plans. As figure 3 illustrates, Fidelity Investments data show that about 40 percent of large plans had adopted automatic enrollment by March 2009, while only about 14 percent of small plans had done so.[25] According to Fidelity's data, about 47 percent of all plan participants are included in plans that offer automatic enrollment.

Plan sponsors can choose to apply automatic enrollment "broadly" to all employees, or more narrowly to include only newly hired employees. Data from Fidelity Investments indicate that automatic enrollment policies are typically applied only to new or recently hired employees, but a growing percentage of plan sponsors extended automatic enrollment to existing employees as well. Among plans with automatic enrollment polices, about 58 percent of plans apply such policies to new and recently hired employees only, while about 42 percent apply automatic enrollment to existing eligible employees as well. [26] There is considerable variation in this pattern by plan size—as figure 3 illustrates, the majority of large plans had adopted automatic enrollment only for new or recently hired employees, while nearly half of small plans applied the policy to all eligible employees.

According to plan sponsors, retirement plan experts, and others we contacted, several considerations have been driving the increase in automatic enrollment. These considerations include: (1) plan sponsors' desire to increase participation rates, (2) plan administrators' marketing of automatic enrollment, and (3) aspects of the Pension Protection Act that facilitate and encourage the adoption of automatic enrollment.

Sponsor Desire to Increase Participation Rates: Officials of each of the six plan sponsors we contacted that had adopted automatic enrollment highlighted the desire to better ensure adequate retirement savings for employees. Some plan sponsors noted that automatic enrollment was considered necessary because other methods of increasing plan participation had not been effective. For example, one plan sponsor had sent e-mails and educational materials reminding employees of the plan's availability and provided them with analyses of the matching funds they had lost by not contributing. While these methods raised contribution rates from the 50 percent range to the 65 percent range, the company could not further increase contribution rates. However, after instituting an automatic enrollment policy, the plan's participation rates increased to 93 percent. An official of another plan sponsor noted that an automatic enrollment policy was necessary because the company had a very young workforce, and the company believed that retirement savings was a very low priority and a distant, "abstract" benefit for these workers. Some plan sponsors also noted that adoption of an automatic enrollment policy may be particularly urgent in the case of plans that discontinue other benefits. For example, representatives of two plan sponsors stated that automatic enrollment was adopted at about the time that an existing defined benefit plan was frozen—that is, closed to new entrants. A representative of a large plan consulting firm noted that sponsors may do this with the long term in view; they want their employees to be able to retire at retirement age, partly to ensure that as productivity drops off, these workers do not have a reason to stay on indefinitely. This plan consultant also said that some plans may adopt automatic enrollment to help ensure that the sponsor can pass nondiscrimination testing.[27]

Plan Administrator Marketing: 401(k) plan administrators—firms that provide and manage retirement plans for plan sponsors—have been actively marketing and promoting adoption of automatic enrollment, according to plan administrators and others. One large plan administrator stated that it encourages automatic enrollment by conducting analyses of the effects of automatic enrollment tailored to individual plan sponsor clients. The official stated that when plan sponsors see the potential benefits to employees of automatic enrollment compared to the status quo, about 25 percent of them have adopted automatic enrollment.

The Pension Protection Act: Finally, various aspects of the PPA have facilitated the trend toward automatic enrollment. An official of one of the nation's largest 401(k) plan administrators noted that the criteria and guidelines established in the PPA streamlined and simplified the decision-making process about automatic enrollment and the related plan design features. One consultant noted that the deliberations about the PPA involved considerable industry input and had an "announcement effect" that generated considerable publicity regarding automatic enrollment. Representatives of two plan sponsors said that the PPA safe harbor protection was a consideration in adopting automatic enrollment.[28] One plan had not adopted all of the PPA safe harbor provisions. Instead, it used the safe harbor specifications as a guide in setting features such as a matching contributions and the 3 percent default contribution rate. The other plan sponsor adopted all of the PPA safe harbor provisions.

Factors Limiting the Adoption of Automatic Enrollment

Various factors, including higher costs, management views, concerns about legal and regulatory challenges, and lack of awareness may delay or prevent the adoption of automatic enrollment policies by some plan sponsors.

declined significantly.[35] This trend toward TDFs as a default investment vehicle is corroborated by data from Fidelity Investments, which shows that 96 percent of plans with an automatic enrollment policy used TDFs as of March 2009, up from 57 percent at the end of 2005.[36]

TARGET-DATE FUNDS

Target-date funds (TDF) offer investors certain advantages generally not offered by other types of investment vehicles. TDFs allocate their investments among various asset classes and shift that allocation to more conservative investments as a "target" date approaches. For example, a TDF could be designed for workers expecting to retire many years in the future and would typically have a much greater allocation to equities and a lesser allocation to fixed-income investments. Conversely, a fund designed for workers nearing retirement age would tend to have a greater allocation to fixed-income investments. TDFs thus offer participants a potentially beneficial long- term asset allocation strategy while lowering risks as the participant approaches retirement age.

Source: GAO synthesis of various descriptive literature.

This trend is important in part because recent evidence suggests that participants who are automatically enrolled in plans with target-date fund defaults tend to have a high concentration of their savings in these funds. A recent analysis by the Employee Benefit Research Institute found that workers who were considered to be automatically enrolled in a 401(k) plan were more likely than those who voluntarily joined to invest all their assets in a TDF.[37] The study found that, except for participants in plans with more than 10,000 participants, more than 90 percent of those automatically enrolled in TDFs had all of their allocation in such funds.

While TDFs may help ensure that workers have a more age-appropriate mix of investments, some experts have stated that TDFs may pose certain challenges, as recent events in the financial markets have illustrated. As a result of the 2008 stock market decline, some TDFs designed for those expecting to retire in or around 2010 lost 25 percent or more in value. In light of concerns about a number of issues, including how plan sponsors evaluate, monitor, and use TDFs, in 2008 the Advisory Council on Employee Welfare and Pension Benefit Plans recommended that the U.S. Department of Labor provide more specific guidance regarding the complex nature of TDFs, and outline the methodology that plan fiduciaries should follow in selecting and monitoring them. The Advisory Council also stated that additional education materials would help plan participants become aware of the value and risks of TDFs.[38]

AUTOMATIC IRA AND STATE-ASSISTED RETIREMENT SAVINGS PLAN PROPOSALS COULD IMPROVE ACCESS TO RETIREMENT SAVINGS VEHICLES FOR UNCOVERED WORKERS, BUT EACH PROPOSAL FACES CHALLENGES

In order to promote retirement savings among the 40 percent of the workforce whose employer does not sponsor a plan, members of Congress, in recent years, have introduced bills for federally required “automatic IRAs” that would be implemented nationwide. Automatic IRAs offer the potential benefit of expanding retirement coverage but some have expressed concerns that automatic IRAs may not result in significant retirement savings, and raised questions about the costs of such a program for employers and the federal government. There have also been proposals for state-supported retirement savings programs over the past several years. These state proposals also have the potential to expand retirement coverage, but on a state-by-state basis. Concerns have been expressed regarding the cost of these state proposals, as well as employer and employee interest in such plans, and potential legal barriers.

Automatic IRAs Could Provide Benefits to More Workers, but Its Impact Is Uncertain

A number of existing proposals have described in general terms the concept of an automatic IRA, and they contain common elements.[39] Under the 2006 and 2007 congressional bills for automatic IRAs, employers that do not sponsor a retirement plan would be required to defer a percentage of an employee’s pay to an IRA through payroll deduction, unless the employee opts out. The requirement would apply to all employers with more than 10 employees and who had been in business for at least 2 years, or employers with 100 or more employees regardless of the length of time the employer has been in business. Eligible workers would be those who had worked for an employer for a specified period, were at least 18 years old, and were not eligible to participate in any other qualified retirement plan the employer sponsors. Affected employers could either (1) automatically enroll eligible workers, although employees would be offered the option to affirmatively opt out or (2) require that employees make an explicit yes or no decision on whether to participate; workers not making such a decision would be automatically enrolled (see fig. 6). Employers would then transfer a portion of employees' pay to either a traditional IRA or a Roth IRA through payroll deduction.[40] Employers could elect to send contributions to IRAs of an employer-designated issuer, unless the employee selects his own IRA provider. If neither the employer nor the employee designates a specific IRA provider, the contributions would be deposited into federally designated default accounts.

The automatic IRA is intended to help address the retirement security needs of those not already covered by an employer-sponsored retirement plan. Further, the automatic IRA is designed to extend the benefits of payroll-deduction savings and automatic features of 401(k)s.[41] According to some experts, requiring employers to offer automatic IRAs is necessary for a number of reasons. First, employers have had the option to establish payroll-deduction IRAs for over 10 years, and for a number of reasons, very few employers have done so. As we previously reported,[42] IRA providers have told us some employers may be reluctant to adopt a payroll-deduction IRA because they believe that their publicizing the payroll-deduction IRAs may be construed as an endorsement of the policy, which could potentially violate ERISA.[43] Further, employers may not be aware of how payroll-deduction IRAs work and some small employers may not be aware that this option exists. The automatic enrollment component is necessary, according to designers of the automatic IRA, because various impediments would prevent many eligible employees from taking advantage of an available payroll-deduction IRA. For example, employees would have to decide whether to participate, select an IRA provider, select investment vehicles, and determine how much to contribute. These officials note that many workers may have difficulty overcoming inertia, and automatic enrollment would help them overcome this difficulty.

Impact on Employees and Retirement Savings

Advocates for automatic IRAs and some pension industry experts reported that the automatic IRA could have a positive effect on retirement savings. According to the architects of the approach, automatic IRAs offer a powerful mechanism for accumulating retirement savings through regular payroll deposits that continue automatically. In light of the impact of automatic enrollment polices on participation in 401(k)s, an automatic IRA program that features default automatic enrollment could have a positive impact on participation rates. One study estimated that likely automatic IRA participants include younger, part-time, and lower- or moderate-income workers, as well as workers subject to higher than average job turnover. Advocates stated that automatic IRAs could help these employees overcome inertia since they would no longer need to take the initiative in order to save. Further, two pension industry experts told us that the payroll-deduction nature of automatic IRAs would ensure that employees of affected companies are saving on a regular basis. However, some experts agree that the automatic enrollment component of automatic IRAs has the potential to significantly increase the number of workers saving for retirement by including workers that currently do not have access to an employer-sponsored plan.

Some caution, however, that the benefits resulting from the automatic IRA could be relatively small. A 2009 preliminary analysis funded by the Department of Labor illustrates potential outcomes of two automatic IRA scenarios using specific behavioral assumptions about participation and contribution rates, among other things.[44] The analysis found that the resulting increase in average retirement benefits at age 70 is small (even when ignoring account fees and offsetting reductions in other savings) and is weighted toward the third of the population with the highest lifetime earnings. If actual participation rates in the automatic IRA are higher than the analysis assumes—and the experience of automatic enrollment in 401(k)s indicates this is a possibility—the resulting increase in average retirement benefits could be higher. The Department of Labor is undertaking additional analysis to illustrate the effects of participation rates similar to those achieved in 401(k) plans with automatic enrollment.

Participants may also not fully benefit from the tax incentives provided by automatic IRAs. According to analysis sponsored by AARP, 50 percent of automatic IRA participants would be lower-income. Therefore, with the exception of Social Security and Medicare taxes, they would pay little, if any, income tax and may not benefit from the tax incentives traditional IRAs offer. Further, while some participants would be eligible for the Saver's Credit, one analysis estimated that the benefit of the credit could be limited. Because the credit is nonrefundable, it can only be used to offset income tax liability. If the participant does not have income tax liability up to the full amount of the credit, the full value of the credit can not be used. For example, the study concluded that if participants made the maximum permitted contributions to an automatic IRA, then nearly 90 percent would not receive the full credit. In part to improve the tax incentive of automatic IRAs, the Department of Treasury, in August of 2009, proposed making the Saver's Credit fully refundable and depositing it automatically into IRAs.[45]

Finally, proper administration of accounts, including record keeping, will be important for managing and maintaining the retirement savings accumulated through the IRAs, according to some analyses and experts. For example, workers would be responsible for ensuring that they do not exceed applicable limits on annual contributions to an automatic IRA. An analysis sponsored by AARP and pension industry officials noted that it might be difficult for some workers to keep track of their accounts when they move from job to job or if their employer goes out of business.[46] A 2007 study noted that automatic IRA proposals do not impose record- keeping responsibilities on employers, beyond withholding and transmitting IRA contributions. Because of this, the report noted that other entities must assume these responsibilities, and a companion report recommended a centralized administrator be responsible for record keeping. For example, the first report found that a central administrator could help prevent lost accounts by providing participants with annual reports including their contributions and investment earnings for the year, as well as the total account balance. In addition, the architects of the automatic IRA proposed that the federal government set up a standard default account and contract with private financial institutions for record- keeping services, among other things, to make managing the IRAs easier.

Impact on Employers

A variety of views exist regarding the cost and administrative burden that an automatic IRA would place on affected small employers. As one analysis of the automatic IRA concept noted, an automatic IRA has the potential to result in some costs and administrative burdens on small employers. The analysis noted that employers would need to provide employees with election forms and process paperwork with respect to employee elections or non-elections, choose an IRA provider or opt for the federally designated default investment, and withhold contributions from employees' pay. Pension industry officials also stated that some small employers do not have payroll deduction systems and send paper or spreadsheet files to their record keepers and brokers. They told us that these employers may choose to invest in new infrastructure in order to remit automatic IRA contributions through payroll deduction.

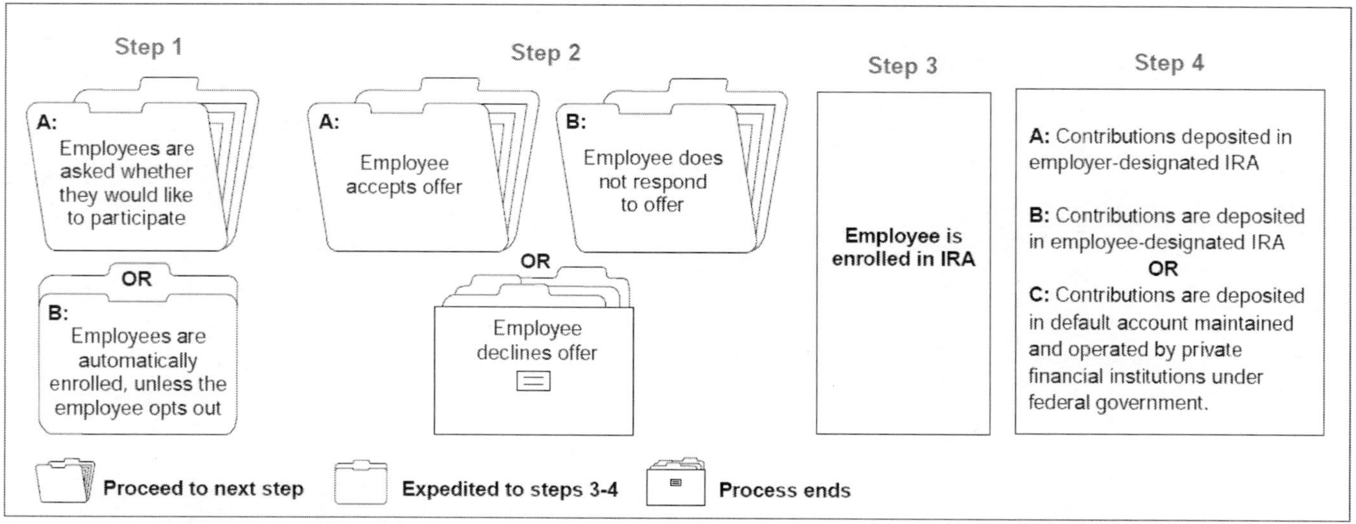

Source: GAO, Adobe systems incorporated.

Figure 6. Steps Involved with Establishing an Automatic IRA.

Recent legislative proposals for an automatic IRA have recognized the potential challenges for small employers and contain provisions to mitigate their impacts. For example, the 2007 bills to authorize automatic IRAs would have exempted employers with fewer than 10 employees as well as those that had been in business for less than 2 years. According to some advocates, the proposals would have therefore avoided placing additional requirements on the smallest companies, which may not have electronic payroll-deduction systems. It would also relieve employers starting a new business from additional costs and administrative burdens. In addition, the proposals would establish a tax credit in the early years for participating employers with fewer than 100 employees to mitigate some administrative and startup costs.

In light of these automatic IRA features, some experts and a recent analysis have found that additional costs may be small for most small employers. The architects of the automatic IRA concept have stated that because many employers already make deductions for federal income tax and payroll tax withholdings, making IRA payroll deductions would impose little, if any, new administrative costs. Further, they said these employers would not have to bear the costs involved in maintaining a retirement plan, such as matching employee contributions. These views were supported by a 2009 report sponsored by AARP, which found that most small employers would face low costs to implement the automatic IRA.[47] This study noted, for example, that about 97 percent of employers with 10 or more employees had automated payroll systems, and such employers would face relatively few burdens implementing the automatic IRA. The report also found that payroll software companies and payroll service providers are likely to adopt automatic IRA requirements in their services to small employers. For the estimated 3 percent of affected employers that process payroll manually, the automatic IRA would also have to be implemented manually.

Impact on the Federal Government

Past proposals have described a federal role that could mitigate some of the difficulties and risks of implementing an automatic IRA. For example, the proposals would have created a new federal entity that would, among other things, establish low-cost default investments.[48] According to experts we contacted and analyses we reviewed, establishing an automatic IRA policy would require tax incentives to make it more affordable to some employers and federal expenditures to establish and govern the program, among other things.[49] However, analyses sponsored by AARP found that it is not possible to determine what the costs would be to the federal government without a more detailed proposal. Further, these studies reported that the establishment of an automatic IRA would reduce federal tax revenues as a result of the tax credit available to small employers, individual tax benefits from deferred employee income, and greater use of the Saver's Credit. Two analyses estimated that the revenue losses could amount to somewhere between $2 billion and $19 billion over 10 years.

Impact on 401(k) Plans

Industry officials and some experts we contacted also noted that establishment of an automatic IRA could affect the market for 401(k) plans. For example, some pension industry experts and representatives of two national organizations representing large plan sponsors noted that if automatic IRAs are made too attractive, they might displace 401(k)s and Savings Incentive Match Plan for Employees of Small Employers (SIMPLE) plans.[50] These officials said that an employer might forego adopting a 401(k) plan if they have already been required to facilitate an automatic IRA, and that this would be unfortunate because an IRA is in many ways an inferior option for workers. The officials told us that a 401(k) plan can offer workers better benefits, such as an employer match and higher contribution rates.[51] In addition, some of the officials reported that the existence of a 401(k) creates a workplace culture that encourages participation in retirement saving. Further, an AARP-sponsored analysis noted that small businesses will weigh the costs of establishing or maintaining a qualified retirement plan against the costs of complying with the automatic IRA requirements. To the extent that the automatic IRA approach offers significantly lower costs—including the relative costs of fiduciary liability—employers may decide against adopting a 401(k) plan or may eliminate an existing one.[52] In light of concerns such as these, officials of one large financial services firm said that, if implemented, the automatic IRA program should be evaluated to determine if it led to a shift away from 401(k) plans.

Others, however, have stated that the automatic IRA is not likely to erode the popularity of 401(k) plans, and may even promote greater adoption of such retirement vehicles. Some experts noted that the potential for automatic IRAs to supplant 401(k)s can be minimized by careful design of the program. Perhaps most importantly, they said that the maximum annual savings for an automatic IRA should be designed so that it is less attractive to a small business employer than a 401(k). Specifically, they noted that it is important that the automatic IRA not permit contributions above the current IRA dollar limits to avoid competing with qualified plans. These advocates reason that the potential tax advantage of a 401(k) enables a small business owner—who, along with his employees, may choose to participate in the 401(k) or IRA plan his business sponsors—to save a much higher percentage of his tax-deferred income than does an automatic IRA, making the 401(k) plan a more attractive option. Further, some industry experts told us that an automatic IRA would likely be a stepping stone toward adopting a 401(k) for some small employers. For example, according to an official of one large organization representing pension professionals stated that payroll deduction automatic IRA arrangements will ultimately encourage more employers to sponsor 401(k) plans, and contribute on their employees' behalf.

State-Assisted Retirement Savings Proposals Intend to Increase Retirement Plan Savings but Raise Questions Regarding Participation, Program Design, and Legal Barriers

In recent years, 10 states have considered proposals that would involve state governments in facilitating retirement savings plans for workers whose employer does not sponsor a plan.[53] One study on such state proposals reported that employers would like to provide a retirement savings vehicle for their employees, but are inhibited by the cost, complexity, and time that would be required to do so.

Under the proposals, state governments could take a number of actions to help address some of these issues and facilitate the use of payroll- deduction or SIMPLE IRAs or the adoption of 401(k) plans. For example, a state would promote private pension coverage and facilitate retirement savings for small business, moderate-income, and lower-income workers—who are less likely to be covered by an employer-sponsored plan—by acting as an intermediary between employers and financial institutions. In addition, a state could help small employers pool their investments and administrative activities.

The type of retirement plans that would be established by the programs varies. For example, California's proposal would establish a payroll-deduction, traditional, or SIMPLE IRA, or a combination of these options; Connecticut's proposal would establish a 401(k) or other type of defined contribution plan; and proposals in Maryland and Washington would establish a defined contribution plan and IRA options.[54] Regardless, the state would initiate and oversee the programs, while private-sector companies under contract to the state would manage the investment vehicles and day-to-day administration. For example, a Washington study outlined an option under which the state would design the basic features of a 401(k) plan and market the plan to private-sector employers who do not currently offer a plan. The state would then contract with a private- sector plan administrator to provide access to investment funds, direct customer service, Web-based account access, and to distribute account statements and other communications. Table 2 shows examples of state roles and the intended impact of automatic IRAs under existing proposals.

Challenges States Would Face

Program Participation: Little is known about the extent to which employers and employees would participate in a state-assisted retirement savings program. According to representatives of two organizations in favor of state-assisted retirement savings plans, employer and employee interest in such a program could be considerable. Moreover, one of the representatives noted that proposals in Washington and other states have been specifically designed to address small companies' concerns that the cost of setting up payroll deduction prevents them from adopting a 401(k) plan or a payroll-deduction IRA. However, no known rigorous assessment exists of the extent to which small employers or employees would opt to participate in such a program. We obtained state-sponsored studies from three of the four states we examined, and while none of the studies included an analysis measuring the magnitude of the market demand for such a program, two noted concerns regarding the potential demand for a state program. For example, a study prepared for the Maryland legislature compared a Maryland proposal to a number of other state financial programs, such as a state-sponsored college savings program.[55] In comparing the two, the report noted that the college savings program offers distinctive tax and pre-payment guarantee advantages that are not otherwise available in the private market. However, the study noted that this distinction, which helps ensure a market demand for the college savings plans, would not exist for the state-assisted retirement program. The report noted that there will be no additional employee tax benefit for participants in the proposed state-assisted retirement savings program and, for that reason, the program would have to compete on an equal footing with plans in the marketplace. The Maryland analysis concluded that the program might be difficult to establish or market in the absence of a federal requirement that all employers have a retirement savings plan.

Table 2. Examples of State Roles and Intended Impact under Existing Proposals

Potential state role	Intended impact
Publicize program and provide information to employers	Through outreach and marketing, the state could inform smaller employers abut the availability and benefits of 401(k) plans or payroll-deduction IRAs. As a result, small employers would become aware of the state program and the benefits their employees would derive from participation.
Develop, approve, and help market a prototype 401(k) plan	A prototype plan document would facilitate employer participation by eliminating a potentially high up-front cost. Such a document could be developed using in-house expertise in coordination with private-sector financial firms.
Negotiate on behalf of small employers and contract with service providers	The state would have bargaining power with financial service providers in light of the prospect that the program could grow to large scale. For example, through competitive bidding the state could negotiate for services that are low in cost and incorporate best practices.
Pool savings of employees of small employers	By facilitating the pooled savings of numerous small accounts, the state would obtain lower-cost retirement plans. Small employers are less likely to sponsor retirement plans in part because of higher per capita costs and because financial service providers are less likely to be interested in serving small accounts.
Assist employers with plan administration and compliance	By providing participating small employers with convenient and professional assistance with plan investments, administrative tasks, and compliance, the state would further encourage small employers to adopt a plan or facilitate a payroll-deduction IRA.

Source: GAO analysis.

Representatives of the financial services industry also indicated that state-assisted programs to some extent could have a “zero-sum” effect. In commentary on the Connecticut proposal in March of 2008, the Small Business Council of America (SBCA) and American Society of Pension Professionals and Actuaries (ASPPA) stated that low-cost retirement options exist now, and the state-assisted program would result in little difference in cost. The SBCA and ASPPA added that state government should not compete with small private businesses unless there is a clear market failure or some inherent unfairness that disadvantages its citizens. Representatives of the Connecticut Bankers Association were concerned that rather than expand retirement savings vehicles to new employees, the state program would attract the "already served market" with initial low costs. Similarly, an SBCA representative stated that providing retirement services to small employers is not very profitable for financial services firms, and if such a proposal resulted in the state obtaining half of the small business market, for example, it is conceivable that large plan administrators would exit the business since they only profit in this sector though large volume. Further, a fiscal analysis of a Washington state proposal noted that the program would have no initial plan assets and uncertain levels of participation and, as a result, vendors may have difficulty estimating the total cost of record-keeping services. This, in turn, could affect vendor interest in providing services for the program.

Table 3. Estimated Program Development and Operation Costs in Washington State

Cost category	Examples	Estimated costs[a]
Program development and ongoing administration	• Working with a contracted defined contribution consultant: • Develop program design • Conduct procurement process for obtaining record keeper and vendors • Create communication plans • Test systems, processes, and communications materials • Provide oversight of program, including legal support and analysis, contract management, and financial reporting	$2,224,000
Communication and marketing	• Develop statewide marketing and communication program targeted toward employers and employees • Publish and disseminate participant and employer communications through mailings and other media such as TV, radio, and Web	$1,606,000
Record keeping	• Contract with third-party record keeper to provide record-keeping service, including: • Daily valuations of participant accounts • Quarterly statements • Customized Web site • Internet account access	$575,000
Total		**$4,405,500**

Source: Fiscal Note to Washington Senate Bill 5791.

[a] Cost estimates are for 2009-2011. The estimate indicated that comparable total costs would also be incurred in future years.

Program Design and Costs to State: Studies from California, Maryland, and Washington about the feasibility of state-assisted retirement savings programs identified important questions about program design and related costs. For example, state governments will need to determine the extent to which administrative and management responsibilities will be borne by the state, and how much will be contracted out to financial services providers. States would also need to determine what types of investment funds will be used, including any default funds. Further, analyses from the three states showed they would face initial and ongoing costs. In addition, a fiscal analysis of the Washington proposal identified three major costs categories—including program development and administration, communications and marketing, and record keeping. As table 3 illustrates, the Washington analysis estimated a total cost of about $4.4 million to implement and operate the program in the first 2 years.

Lack of startup funding may be a significant barrier in some states. While the Maryland and Connecticut proposals allow for state budget appropriations (which may later be recovered through participant fees), the California proposal stated that initial funding could come from a state budget appropriation or a non-profit or private entity. However, state budget appropriations may be difficult to obtain given these states' current budget shortfalls. The Washington proposal stated that its program could not be started until the state had obtained federal and/or philanthropic funds sufficient to support the first 3 years of the program. According to an advocate for the Washington proposal, his organization recognized that, due to the current economy, the states are not in a position to self-fund state-assisted retirement savings programs. He reported that his organization has been working on obtaining federal funds to cover the startup costs of such programs.

Legal and Regulatory Challenges: State-assisted savings programs would also have to comply with both federal and state law that, according to the state analyses, could provide additional challenges. One analysis noted that states would need to obtain requisite federal approvals to ensure that the programs adhere to all federal requirements governing the operation of retirement plans. For example, if the program establishes 401(k) accounts, the state would need to submit plan documents to the IRS and Department of Labor for approval. Further, the Maryland and Washington analyses found that if a state sponsored the establishment of a 401(k) plan, such plans would be subject to ERISA's fiduciary requirements and expose either the state or the employer to potential liability in the event that participants suffer financial losses. According to the Maryland analysis, participants may try to hold the state or the employer liable if they incur investment losses after being sold an investment unsuitable for their needs or if they received misleading communications about investments. However, both analyses noted that there are steps the states can take to minimize their liability. For example, according to the Maryland study, the state could limit investment options to reduce the possibility of unsuitable choices or miscommunication.

The Washington and Maryland analyses discussed a number of other potential liabilities that states could face. For example, the Maryland analysis noted that a failure to file required forms and conduct transactions under applicable standards could subject the state or employers to significant penalties imposed by IRS or the Department of Labor. Officials from Washington noted that a 401(k) option could create a new and complex compliance and monitoring role for the state retirement agency and that it could be administratively difficult for the state to assume this role. They added that the state would face a steep learning curve in addressing ERISA and liability issues, and might have to contract with outside expertise to deal with compliance and oversight issues.

The state role envisioned in the proposals may be precluded by some states' constitutions. Analyses of proposals in California and Washington specifically cited aspects of the state constitutions that could affect the states' ability to operate a plan. For example, California's constitution prohibits the gift or loan of state credit to associations, companies or corporations, and prohibits the state from loaning its credit, subscribing to, or being interested in the stock of any company, association, or corporation.[56] According to the California study, although California's constitution specifically exempts the retirement board of a public retirement system from this prohibition, it is not clear whether the exemption would extend to a program for private-sector employees. The California study noted that if the program is structured in such a way that the state internally manages funds associated with the program, this could be seen as the state having a financial interest outside the limits of the public employees' retirement fund. The California study also observed that a constitutional amendment may be needed to address this issue. Washington's constitution has a similar prohibition.[57] The Washington report noted that the proposed retirement savings program may be permissible because it serves a public purpose by helping individuals save for retirement and reducing the risk that individuals will rely on state assistance in the absence of adequate retirement savings. However, the report also noted that no Washington case has considered proposals similar to those discussed in the report. The report concluded that it was not possible to predict how a court would rule should the program be challenged. In addition, because no other states have enacted such programs, there is no guidance available from other courts.

Concluding Observations

Automatic enrollment of workers in 401(k) plans has proven to be an effective means of increasing plan participation rates. Because such policies are being increasingly adopted by defined contribution plan sponsors in the wake of the Pension Protection Act of 2006, many additional workers will be brought into plans who might not otherwise have participated. Nonetheless, a number of considerations could potentially limit the extent or impact of such policies. First, the benefits of automatic enrollment are inherently limited to workers that have access to an employer-sponsored plan but do not participate. Second, some types of employers, such as employers with high-turnover workforces and small employers, may find automatic enrollment too costly or inappropriate for their workforce. Third, initially low default contribution rates and the absence of default automatic escalation policies at some plans may result in inadequate long-term savings for some workers.

Automatic IRAs may hold promise for workers who do not have access to an employer-sponsored plan. The proposal has potential in that it could foster retirement savings among the roughly 40 percent of the workforce whose employers do not sponsor a plan. As such a policy is designed, however, a number of important issues remain to be considered. For example, it is not clear that an automatic IRA will offer low-income workers a significant benefit. Further, in order to ensure that the intended beneficiaries accumulate and retain savings, some central administration—possibly by the federal government—may be required to assume significant and long-term involvement for record keeping and administration. The nature and costs of such a role have not yet been publicly assessed or compared against the potential benefits and limitations of an automatic IRA. In addition, while state-assisted retirement savings plans may also hold some promise for expanding retirement coverage for workers, none of these proposals has been enacted and they could face significant legal barriers to implementation.

Both the growth of automatic enrollment and the introduction of automatic IRA proposals have brought renewed attention to the question of how to extend retirement coverage to the half of the workforce not covered by an employer-sponsored plan. This is an important step forward, as past debate over retirement security has largely focused on increasing retirement savings for those already participating in retirement plans. As plan sponsors and participants gain more experience with automatic enrollment, it will be helpful to learn from these experiences, especially in light of the recent recession. The lessons learned may have important implications for related 401(k) plan features, such as automatic escalation, and for the potential feasibility and usefulness of automatic IRA and state-assisted retirement savings proposals. Further, it would also be helpful to carefully consider the various concerns raised in the automatic IRA debate to increase the likelihood that, if such a proposal becomes law, it is administered in an efficient and effective way. Finally, while state efforts could be helpful in increasing the number of workers saving for retirement, these efforts may not be necessary depending on the potential implementation of automatic IRAs. Further, fiscal difficulties in some states may make such proposals difficult to implement in the near future.

AGENCY COMMENTS

We provided a draft of this report to the Department of Labor and the Department of the Treasury for review and comment. The Department of Labor generally agreed with our findings. With regard to the potential impacts of an automatic IRA on retirement benefits, Labor said that the Employee Benefits Security Administration is undertaking additional analysis to illustrate the effect of higher participation rates, similar to those achieved in 401(k) plans. The Department of Labor provided technical comments, which we incorporated as appropriate.

The Department of the Treasury also generally agreed with our findings, and provided technical comments, which we incorporated as appropriate.

Sincerely yours,

Barbara D. Bovbjerg
Director, Education, Workforce, and Income Security Issues

Appendix I: Scope and Methodology

To determine what is known about the effect of automatic enrollment policies among the nation's defined contribution plans, as well as the extent of and prospects for such policies, we first reviewed reports examining the impact of automatic enrollment, default contribution rates, and default investment funds on participation rates and saving patterns. Table 4 shows the six reports presenting original research that we reviewed.

Officials at the Department of Labor, as well as other pension industry experts, verified our selections. The six reports include two conducted by large plan administrators that analyzed the records of their respective defined contribution plan sponsors and participants. The remaining four reports conducted case studies of companies that adopted automatic enrollment and analyzed participation rates, contribution rates, and investment fund allocations before and after the policy was implemented. For each study, we analyzed available evidence on: (1) the impact of automatic enrollment on participation rates and the durability of any increases in participation, (2) the characteristics of the workers whose participation rates are affected by automatic enrollment,(3) the impact of automatic enrollment on contribution rates, and (4) the impact of automatic enrollment on selection of investment funds. However, the findings of these case studies may not be generalizable for three reasons. First, each study examined the experience of only one to three companies. Second, many of the companies in the four case studies seem to have been facing difficulty meeting nondiscrimination testing requirements. Third, some offered matching contributions to their employees and it is unclear whether the presence of a match affects automatic enrollment participation rates. Therefore, the experiences of these companies may not be representative of all 401(k) sponsors.

To determine the extent to which plans had adopted automatic enrollment policies, we obtained data from two large plan administrators—Fidelity Investment and Vanguard Investments. Data from Fidelity represents the 18,100 qualified defined contribution plans Fidelity administers, encompassing about 14 million plan participants and over $600 billion in assets. Data from Vanguard is drawn from Vanguard's universe of defined contribution plans—more than 2,200 qualified plans that encompass more than 3 million participants and almost $200 billion in assets. We determined that these data accurately reflect the experience of Fidelity and Vanguard, but are not necessarily representative of the universe of defined contribution plans.

Table 4. Six Studies We Reviewed on the Impact of Automatic Enrollment and Related Policies

Study	Authors (year of study)
Measuring the Effectiveness of Automatic Enrollment	Vanguard Center for Retirement Research (2007)
For Better or For Worse	Choi et al. (2001)
Nationwide Savings Plan Automatic Enrollment Getting Associates PREPared for Retirement	Swanson and Farnen (2008)
The Power of Suggestion	Madrian and Shea (2001)
Building Futures Volume VIII	Fidelity Investments (2007)
The Importance of Default Options for Retirement Saving Outcomes: Evidence from the United States	Beshears et al. (2008)

Source: GAO.

We conducted in-depth interviews with 12 plan sponsors to obtain their perspectives on their experiences with automatic enrollment and related policies, as well as prospects for the policies. We used Form 5500 data from the Department of Labor to select a sample that included plan sponsors from a variety of industries including those that may be considered to have low wages and high turnover, and vice-versa, and small, medium, and large plans, as measured by number of participants. Six of the plan sponsors had adopted automatic enrollment, including one that had significantly narrowed the scope of its automatic enrollment policy, two that had adopted a 401(k) plan within the past 5 years, and 10 that have sponsored a 401(k) plan for more than 5 years. The remaining six plan sponsors have not adopted automatic enrollment. Table 5 shows the industries and plan sponsor sizes for the 12 sponsors that we contacted.

In addition, we conducted interviews with officials at the Departments of the Treasury and Labor, as well as academic experts from the Employee Benefits Research Institute (EBRI), Brookings, The Heritage Foundation, Harvard University, and the New School of Social Research. We also interviewed 401(k) plan administrators, providers, and consultants including Deloitte, Fidelity Investments, Vanguard, Mercer, Watson Wyatt, T. Rowe Price, ADP, State Street Global Advisors, and Renaissance Institutional Management. Finally, we interviewed industry and research organizations such as the Investment Company Institute (ICI), the Pension Rights Center (PRC), AARP, the Profit Sharing/401(k) Council of America (PSCA), the

American Benefits Council (ABC), American Society for Pension Professionals and Actuaries (ASPPA), the Center for American Progress (CAP), the AFL-CIO, the Small Business Council of America (SBCA), and the Committee on Investment of Employee Benefit Assets (CIEBA).

Table 5. Industries and Plan Sponsor Sizes

Industry	Number of plan sponsors
Professional and business services	1
Utilities	1
Manufacturing	2
Accommodation and food services	1
Arts, entertainment, and recreation	1
Transportation and warehousing	1
Information	1
Finance and insurance	2
Retail trade	2
Plan size	
Small (<150 employees)	3
Medium (150-4,999 employees)	3
Large (>5,000 employees)	6

Source: GAO analysis of Form 5500 data from the Department of Labor.

To determine the potential benefits and limitations of automatic IRA proposals and state-assisted retirement savings plan proposals, we analyzed the Automatic IRA Acts of 2006 and 2007 as well as state-assisted retirement savings proposals from four states. The Economic Opportunity Institute identified nine states that have introduced state-assisted retirement savings proposals: California, Connecticut, Maryland, Massachusetts, Michigan, Pennsylvania, Rhode Island, Vermont, Virginia, and Washington.[58] In addition, the architect of the state-assisted retirement savings concept identified Vermont as having introduced a proposal. We selected four—California, Connecticut, Maryland, and Washington—for an in-depth review because these states covered a range of plan type offerings and we were able to obtain feasibility studies or testimony prepared for state congressional hearings on their proposals. We did not conduct an independent legal review of these proposals. We analyzed the work of two researchers from Brookings and The Heritage Foundation that have developed proposals for the automatic IRA and state-assisted retirement savings plans. We then reviewed four studies sponsored by AARP examining the feasibility of automatic IRAs; survey reports by AARP and Prudential on employee and employer attitudes toward automatic IRAs; a microsimulation analysis of the impact of automatic IRAs on workers' savings accumulations and retirement security; and three feasibility studies on California, Maryland, and Washington states' proposals. In addition, we reviewed testimony and written materials from hearings held in Connecticut and Washington to obtain the perspectives of state officials, small business representatives, and pension industry representatives on state-assisted retirement savings proposals. We also reviewed relevant federal laws and regulations.

We interviewed researchers who have focused on the topic, including those from Brookings, The Heritage Foundation, EBRI, the Economic Opportunity Institute, Harvard University, and the New School for Social Research as well as officials from AARP, PSCA, ASPPA, CIEBA, ABC, ICI, CAP, and PRC. In addition, we interviewed state officials from Washington, Maryland, and California as well as officials from pension plan administrators and consultants, including Mercer, Watson Wyatt, T. Rowe Price, ADP, State Street Global Advisors, and Renaissance Institutional Management. Finally, we interviewed a 401(k) consultant for small businesses and an official from SBCA to obtain the perspective of representatives of the small business community.

SELECTED BIBLIOGRAPHY ON AUTOMATIC ENROLLMENT

Beshears, John, James J., Choi, David Laibson & Brigitte C. Madrian. (2008). "The Importance of Default Options for Retirement Saving Outcomes: Evidence from the USA." Chapter 3 in *Lessons from Pension Reform in the Americas*, edited by Stephen J. Kay and Tapen Sinha. New York: Oxford University Press Inc.

Copeland, Craig. (2009). *Use of Target-Date Funds in 401(k) Plans*, 2007. Issue Brief 327. Washington, D.C.: Employee Benefits Research Institute, March.

Fidelity Investments. (2008). *Building Futures: Auto Solutions Data*. Boston, Mass.: September.

—. *Building Futures Volume VIII: A Report on Corporate Defined Contribution Plans*. Boston, Mass.: 2007.

Choi, James J., David Laibson, Brigitte C. Madrian, & Andrew Metrick. (2004). "For Better or For Worse: Default Effects and 401(k) Savings

Behavior." Chapter 2 in *Perspectives on the Economics of Aging*, edited by David A. Wise. Chicago: University of Chicago Press, June.

—. "Saving for Retirement on the Path of Least Resistance." Chapter 11 in *Behavioral Public Finance*, edited by Edward J. McCaffery and Joel Slemrod. New York, N.Y.: Russell Sage Foundation, 2006.

Madrian, Brigitte C. & Dennis F. Shea. (2001). "The Power of Suggestion: Inertia in 401(k) Participation and Savings Behavior." *The Quarterly Journal of Economics*, vol. CXVI, no. 4 (November), 1149-1187.

Mitchell, Olivia S. & Stephen P. Utkus. (2004). "Lessons from Behavioral Finance for Retirement Plan Design." Chapter 1 in *Pension Design and Structure New Lessons from Behavioral Finance*, edited by Olivia S. Mitchell and Stephen P. Utkus. New York, N.Y.: Oxford University Press Inc.

Nessmith, William E., Stephen P. Utkus, & Jean A. Young. (2007). *Measuring the Effectiveness of Automatic Enrollment*. Valley Forge, Pa.: Vanguard Center for Retirement Research, December.

Swanson, Mark D. and D. Bryan Farnen. "Nationwide Savings Plan Automatic Enrollment Getting Associates PREPared for Retirement." *Benefits Quarterly*, vol. *24*, no. 3 (Third Quarter 2008): 13-19.

End Notes

[1] See GAO, *Private Pensions: Low Defined Contribution Plan Savings May Pose Challenges to Retirement Security, Especially for Many Low-Income Workers*, GAO-08-8 (Washington, D.C.: November 2007), p. 3.

[2] The Current Population Survey is a monthly survey conducted by the U.S. Census Bureau among a nationally representative sample of approximately 100,000 households, primarily in order to estimate the rates of employment and unemployment. During March of each year, the survey includes supplemental questions about retirement plan participation and other financial matters.

[3] Patrick Purcell, *Retirement Plan Participation and Contributions: Trends from 1998 to 2006.* (Washington, D.C.: Congressional Research Service, Jan. 30, 2009). This report is based on an analysis of the Survey of Income and Program Participation (SIPP), which is conducted by the U.S. Census Bureau and encompasses a nationally representative sample of the civilian, noninstitutionalized population of the United States. The SIPP is a longitudinal survey, which means that it measures changes pertaining to the same individuals and households over time.

[4] Brady, Peter, and Stephen Sigrist, *Who Gets Retirement Plans and Why*, Investment Company Institute Perspective 14, no. 2 (Washington D.C.: September 2008).

[5] In some other types of defined contribution plans, such as profit-sharing and money- purchase plans, all workers are typically included in the plan, and the employer makes contributions and often invests the money in the employees' account.

[6] A plan must be considered "qualified" to obtain favorable tax treatment under federal law. One requirement for a qualified 401(k) plan is that participants must elect to have the employer provide an amount of salary to the employee in cash, or to defer the amount of salary and deposit the amount in the employee's plan account.

[7] The 1998 IRS ruling—IRS Revenue Ruling 98-30—held that employer contributions made to a plan on an employee's behalf, in lieu of cash payment, are considered elective contributions, so long as the employee has an opportunity to receive cash instead, and has not affirmatively expressed a desire to do so. In a subsequent ruling—IRS Revenue Ruling 2000-8—the IRS determined that contributions made on behalf of either a newly hired or current employee in lieu of cash compensation were valid elective contributions.

[8] Pub. L. No. 109-280 (2006) §902 of PPA added Code sections 401(k)(13), 401(m)(12) and 414(w). See final regulations of the Internal Revenue Service regarding "Automatic Contribution Arrangements" at 74 Fed. Reg. 8200 (Feb. 24, 2009).

[9] These IRS actions include Revenue Ruling 2009-30, which demonstrates ways a 401(k) plan sponsor can include automatic contribution increases in its plan, and Notice 2009-65, which includes sample automatic enrollment plan language that a 401(k) plan sponsor can adopt with automatic IRS approval.

[10] IRAs were established under the Employees Retirement Income Security Act of 1974. (Pub. L. 93-406, codified at 29 U.S.C. 1001 et seq.) IRAs are intended to provide individuals not covered by employer-sponsored retirement plans an opportunity to save for retirement in their own tax-deferred accounts, and to give retiring workers or those changing jobs a way to preserve assets in employer-sponsored plans by allowing them to transfer plan balances to an IRA. Over the past 30 years, Congress has created several types of IRAs with different features for individuals and small businesses.

[11] The two legislative proposals were the Automatic IRA Act of 2007, S. 1141 and H.R. 2167, 110th Cong., 1st sess.; and the Automatic IRA Act of 2006, S. 3952 and H.R. 6210, 109th Cong., 2nd sess.

[12] For example, see Wash. Second Substitute Senate Bill 5791, 61st Legislature, 2009 Regular Session, and Md. Senate Bill 728, 2008 Regular Session.

[13] Four of the six analyses we reviewed were case studies that compared participation rates at companies before and after automatic enrollment was adopted, while two of the analyses were conducted by large plan administrators and analyzed the records of their respective defined contribution plan sponsors and participants. Because these analyses do not represent a random sample of 401(k) plan sponsors, their findings are not generalizable. For more information about the studies, see appendix I.

[14] Brigitte C. Madrian and Dennis F. Shea, "The Power of Suggestion: Inertia in 401(k) Participation and Savings Behavior," *The Quarterly Journal of Economics*, vol. CXVI, no. 4: 1149-1187.

[15] Olivia S. Mitchell and Stephen P. Utkus, "Lessons from Behavioral Finance for Retirement Plan Design." Chapter 1 in *Pension Design and Structure: New Lessons from Behavioral Finance*, eds. Olivia S. Mitchell and Stephen P. Utkus. (New York, N.Y.: Oxford University Press Inc., 2004).

[16] James J. Choi, David Laibson, Brigitte C. Madrian, and Andrew Metrick, "Saving for Retirement on the Path of Least Resistance." Chapter 11 in *Behavioral Public Finance*, eds. Edward J. McCaffery and Joel Slemrod. New York: Russell Sage Foundation, 2006.

[17] Madrian and Shea.

[18] Fidelity Investments, *Building Futures Volume VIII: A Report on Corporate Defined Contribution Plans* (Boston, Mass.: 2007). Fidelity compared the participation rate for

automatic enrollment–eligible employees in plans with automatic enrollment with the participation rate for eligible employees in plans without automatic enrollment. The study analyzed the data of more than 10 million participants in nearly 13,000 Fidelity-administered plans, representing $674 billion in assets.

[19] Madrian and Shea.

[20] James J. Choi, David Laibson, Brigitte C. Madrian, and Andrew Metrick, "For Better or For Worse: Default Effects and 401(k) Savings Behavior." Chapter 2 in *Perspectives on the Economics of Aging*, ed. David A. Wise. Chicago: University of Chicago Press, June 2004. John Beshears, James J. Choi, David Laibson, and Brigitte C. Madrian, "The Importance of Default Options for Retirement Saving Outcomes: Evidence from the USA." Chapter 3 in *Lessons from Pension Reform in the Americas*, eds. Stephen J. Kay and Tapen Sinha. (New York: Oxford University Press Inc., 2008).

[21] William E. Nessmith, Stephen P. Utkus, and Jean A. Young, *Measuring the Effectiveness of Automatic Enrollment* (Valley Forge, Pa.: Vanguard Center for Retirement Research, December 2007). Vanguard reported predicted effects from a logistic regression modeling comparing 527 plans with voluntary enrollment and 48 plans that implemented automatic enrollment for new hires only. Plans introducing automatic enrollment during the analysis period have employees hired under both voluntary and automatic enrollment. As of December 31, 2007, Vanguard administered over 2,200 defined contribution plans with more than 3 million participants. A Vanguard official reported that total plan assets at the end of 2008 were approximately $194 billion.

[22] It should be noted that rates of participation in employer-sponsored plans without automatic enrollment tend to increase with the length of employee tenure. For this reason, the impact of automatic enrollment on participation rates may be significantly less pronounced as length of tenure increases.

[23] A money market fund is a type of mutual fund that is required by law to invest in low-risk securities. These funds have relatively low risks compared to other mutual funds. A stable-value fund typically invests in bonds and achieves rates of return 2 to 3 percentage points higher than money market funds. The fund manager guarantees the investors a certain rate of return.

[24] Choi et al. and Madrian and Shea. While particular types of assets, such as money-market and stable-value funds, may result in lower asset accumulations for some participants, they must also consider market risk when assessing their asset allocations. Market risk is the possibility of an overall decline in a broad class of assets, such as stocks. In 2008, stock values fell across the board and even well-diversified portfolios could not protect participants' portfolios from depreciating. Most investment advisors recommend diversifying across asset classes as well as within a particular asset class. For example, bond prices have historically been less volatile than stock prices, and there have been long periods when returns on bonds and stocks have not been closely correlated.

[25] For purposes of this data, Fidelity defines large plans as those with more than $500 million in assets, mid-sized plans as those with between $35 million and $500 million, and small plans as those with less than $35 million in assets.

[26] Fidelity Investments, *Building Futures: Auto Solutions Data* (Boston, Mass.: September 2008).

[27] To maintain their 401(k) plans' qualified status, employers must perform tests to ensure that their plans comply with federal tax nondiscrimination rules (26 U.S.C. §401). These rules seek to balance benefit accruals of highly paid participants with those of non-highly paid participants.

[28] The plan sponsor may utilize a "safe harbor" to avoid otherwise required ADP and ACP antidiscrimination testing of these plans. Specifically, in exchange for utilizing the safe harbor, the employer is required to make certain contributions to plan participants and use an accelerated vesting schedule.

[29] A recent GAO report discusses the impact of lump sum distributions—that is, cashouts of account balances at job separation that are not rolled over into another retirement plan—and other forms of 401(k) account "leakage": 401(k) *Plans: Policy Changes Could Reduce the Long-term Effects of Leakage on Workers' Retirement Savings* GAO-09-715 (Washington, D.C.: Aug. 28, 2009).

[30] While there is no consensus about what constitutes an adequate contribution rate, some pension experts have cited combined contribution rates—including employer and employee contributions—of between 12 and 20 percent of pay.

[31] Interviews with plans sponsors and others revealed a number of reasons for the predominance of the 3 percent default rate. For example, a representative of a firm that consults with many retirement plans stated that plan sponsors do not want a high default contribution rate that would risk causing automatically enrolled participants to drop out of the plan. A large plan administrator noted that the Pension Protection Act's specification of a 3 percent minimum default rate for safe harbor plans was seen by many as implied advice to start at 3 percent.

[32] According to data from Fidelity, another 46 percent of automatic enrollment plans have adopted optional automatic escalation, which means that participants have the option of increasing their contribution rate automatically at periodic intervals, such as once per year.

[33] According to a representative of a plan administrator, a number of factors could explain this difference. For example, one plan administrator may have actively promoted default automatic escalation.

[34] This shift in TDF asset allocation is commonly referred to as the fund's "glide path." Sometimes TDFs have significant equity components at the retirement date and even at the endpoint of the glide path.

[35] Both money market and stable value funds were often used as default investments before the PPA because employers were concerned about legal liability if investments they had chosen declined in value as a result of market fluctuations. As a result, they were led to invest workers contributions in such low-risk, low-return default investments.

[36] Target-date funds are also sometimes referred to as "lifecycle funds." The two are generally synonymous in that they both adjust the proportion of different asset classes over time so that the investor has lower risk as they approach retirement.

[37] Craig Copeland, *Use of Target-Date Funds in 401(k) Plans, 2007*, Issue Brief 327 (Washington, D.C.: Employee Benefit Research Institute, March 2009). This analysis was based on the Employee Benefit Research Institute/Investment Company Institute database, which contains data on nearly 22 million participants in participant-directed retirement plans. Although this database does not include information on plans' use of automatic enrollment, the author of the study developed a proxy to identify participants who were considered to have been automatically enrolled.

[38] The Department of Labor and the Securities and Exchange Commission held a joint public hearing in June 2009 on TDFs and are currently reviewing the testimony presented at the hearing and supplemental materials submitted for the public record. (*Hearing on Target Date Funds and Similar Investment Options*, 74 Fed. Register 24052).

[39] S. 1141 and H.R. 2167, 110th Cong., 1st sess.; S. 3952 and H.R. 6210, 109th Cong., 2nd sess.; David C. John and J. Mark Iwry, *Pursuing Universal Retirement Security Through Automatic Iras*, Joint Written Statement before Subcommittee on Long-Term Growth and

Debt Reduction Committee on Finance, United States Senate. Washington, D.C.: June 29, 2006. The White House's FY 2010 Budget Proposal also called for an automatic workplace pension program. Further, in its August 2009 proposals for financial regulatory reform, the Department of the Treasury called for the enactment of the automatic IRA (The Department of the Treasury, *Financial Regulatory Reform: A New Foundation: Rebuilding Financial Supervision and Regulation* (Washington, D.C.: Aug. 11, 2009)). At this writing, no bill for an automatic IRA had been introduced before the 111th (current) Congress.

[40] A traditional IRA allows individuals to defer taxes on investment earnings accumulated in these accounts until distribution at retirement. A Roth IRA, in contrast, allows employees to make after-tax contributions to an IRA and, after age 59½, take tax-free distributions of their investment earnings. Account owners can also make tax-free withdrawals of their contributions after age 59½, as long as they have held the account for 5 years.

[41] We first reported on the potential benefits of automatic IRAs in our 2007 report *Private Pensions: Low Defined Contribution Plan Savings May Pose Challenges to Retirement Security, Especially for Many Low-Income Workers*, GAO-08-8 (Washington, D.C.: Nov. 29, 2007). We projected DC plan savings assuming that all employees participate immediately, rather than waiting for eligibility or opting not to participate. We found that instant and universal participation not only raised average savings for the sample as a whole, but had a relatively strong impact on workers in the lowest income quartile. Although our projections were for DC plans, they suggested that automatic features intended to increase participation can have a strong impact on retirement savings levels.

[42] See GAO, *Individual Retirement Accounts: Government Actions Could Encourage More Employers to Offer IRAs to Employees*, GAO-08-590 (Washington, D.C.: June 4, 2008).

[43] Employers may establish payroll-deduction IRAs and are not subject to ERISA fiduciary requirements so long as they follow regulations set by the Department of Labor. Further, the Small Business Job Protection Act of 1996, Pub. L. No. 104-188, established SIMPLE IRAs specifically for the purpose of encouraging more employers to sponsor IRAs. SIMPLE IRAs were designed to encourage employers with 100 or fewer employees to assist workers with retirement savings. Under a SIMPLE IRA, an employer can both direct a portion of an employee's salary to an IRA and offer a matching contribution.

[44] This analysis was conducted by the Policy Simulation Group at the request of the Department of Labor. The analysis considers the impact of an automatic IRA fully implemented in 2010 on the annual retirement benefits of individuals aged 70 in the year 2065. The analysis creates a hypothetical birth cohort and models the cohort's lives from birth to death, including all life events such as marriages, births, education and job decisions, pension coverage and behavior, and retirement.

[45] The Department of the Treasury, *Financial Regulatory Reform: A New Foundation: Rebuilding Financial Supervision and Regulation* (Washington, D.C.: Aug. 11, 2009).

[46] Mary M. Schmitt and Judy Xanthopoulos, *Automatic IRAs: Are They Administratively Feasible, What Are the Costs to Employers and the Federal Government, and Will They Increase Retirement Savings?*, Preliminary Report Prepared for AARP (Optimal Benefit Strategies, LLC, Mar. 8, 2007).

[47] *Most Small Employers Face Low Costs to Implement Automatic IRAs*, a report prepared for AARP (Optimal Benefit Strategies, LLC, Aug. 19, 2009).

[48] Although the 2007 House and Senate bills for an automatic IRA included establishment of a governing board modeled on the Federal Thrift Investment Board—a so-called TSP II Board—the bill did not, as the AARP-sponsored analysis noted, clearly delineate the amount of reporting and record keeping that would be required.

[49] For example, the Department of Labor's enforcement activities currently include pursuing 401(k) plan payroll deductions that are not remitted to employees' accounts in a timely manner. Department of Labor officials stated that the government would have to undertake similar activities in instances where automatic IRA payroll deductions are not timely remitted.

[50] An employer with 100 or fewer employees may establish a SIMPLE plan. A SIMPLE plan is a simplified retirement plan for small employers that is not subject to some of the same requirements that the Internal Revenue Code imposes on qualified pension plans.

[51] The 2009 maximum annual tax-favored contribution levels are as follows: $5,000 for a traditional or Roth IRA, $11,500 for a SIMPLE IRA, and $16,500 for a 401(k).

[52] Schmitt and Xanthopoulos 2007.

[53] The 10 states are California, Connecticut, Maryland, Massachusetts, Michigan, Pennsylvania, Rhode Island, Vermont, Virginia, and Washington. We focused our analysis on proposals in four states—California, Connecticut, Maryland, and Washington—because these proposals cover a range of retirement plan options, among other criteria (for more on selection criteria, see app. I).

[54] See Cal. Assembly Bill No. 125, 2009-10 Regular Session; Conn. General Assembly Raised Bill No. 971, January Session, 2009; Md. Senate Bill 728 and House Bill 1228, 2008 Regular Session; Wash. Second Substitute Senate Bill 5791 and House Bill 1893, 61st Legislature, 2009 Regular Session.

[55] Michael Rubenstein, *Maryland Voluntary Employee Accounts Program Study* (Annapolis: January 2008).

[56] CA Const. art. XVI, § 17.

[57] WA Const. art. VIII, § 5 and art. XII, § 9.

[58] The Economic Opportunity Institute is a non-profit public policy organization located in Washington state that focuses on retirement security and several other issues.

In: 401(k) Plans
Editor: Wesley Meyer

ISBN: 978-1-63484-727-8

Chapter 3

Defined Contribution Plans: Key Information on Target Date Funds as Default Investments Should Be Provided to Plan Sponsors and Participants*

United States Government Accountability Office

Why GAO Did This Study

To promote the adoption of appropriate default investments by retirement plans that automatically enroll workers, in 2007 the Department of Labor (DOL) identified three qualified default investment alternatives. One of these options—target date funds (TDF)—has emerged as by far the most popular default investment. TDFs are designed to provide an age-appropriate asset allocation for plan participants over time.

Because of recent concerns about significant losses in and differences in the performance of some TDFs, GAO was asked address the following questions: (1) To what extent do the investment compositions of TDFs vary; (2) what is known about the performance of TDFs; (3) how do plan sponsors select and monitor TDFs that are chosen as the plan's default investment, and

* This is an edited, reformatted and augmented version of the United States Government Accountability Office publication, GAO-11-118, dated January 2011.

what steps do they take to communicate information on these funds to their participants; and (4) what steps have DOL and the Securities and Exchange Commission (SEC) taken to ensure that plan sponsors appropriately select and use TDFs? To answer these questions, GAO reviewed available reports and data, and interviewed TDF managers, plan sponsors, relevant federal officials, and others.

What GAO Recommends

GAO recommends that DOL take actions to assist plan sponsors in selecting TDFs to best suit their employees, and to ensure that plan participants have access to essential information about TDFs. DOL raised a number of issues with our recommendations, and we amended one of them in response to their comments.

What GAO Found

Target date funds vary considerably in asset structures and in other ways, largely as a result of the different objectives and investment philosophies of fund managers. In the years approaching the retirement date, for example, some TDFs have a relatively low equity allocation—35 percent or less—so that plan participants will be insulated from excessive losses near retirement. Other TDFs have an equity allocation of 60 percent or more in the belief that relatively high equity returns will help ensure that retirees do not deplete savings in old age. TDFs also vary considerably in other respects, such as in the use of alternative assets and complex investment techniques. In addition, allocations are based in part on assumptions about plan participant actions—such as contribution rates and how plan participants will manage 401(k) assets upon retirement—which may differ from the actions of many participants. These investment differences and differences between assumed and actual participant behavior may have significant implications for the retirement security of plan participants invested in TDFs.

Recent TDF performance has varied considerably, and while studies show that many investors will obtain significantly positive returns over the long term, a small percentage of investors may have poor or negative returns. Between 2005 and 2009 annualized TDF returns for the largest funds with 5 years of returns ranged from +28 percent to -31 percent. Although TDFs do not have a long history, studies modeling the potential long-term performance of TDFs show that TDFs investment returns may vary greatly. For example, while one study found that the mean rate of return for all individual participants was +4.3 percent, some participant groups could experience significantly lower returns. These studies also found that different ratios of investments affect the range of TDF investment returns and offer various trade-offs.

While some plan sponsors conduct robust TDF selection and monitoring processes, other plan sponsors face challenges in doing so. Plan sponsors and industry experts identified several key considerations in selecting and monitoring TDFs, such as the demographics of participants and the expertise of the plan sponsor. Some plan sponsors may face several challenges in evaluating TDFs, such as having limited resources to conduct a thorough selection process, or lacking a benchmark to meaningfully measure performance. Although plan sponsors may use various media in an effort to inform participants about funds offered through the plan, some plan sponsors and others noted that participants typically understand little about TDFs.

DOL and SEC have taken important steps to improve TDF disclosures, participant education, and guidance for plan sponsors and participants. For example, both agencies have proposed regulations aimed at helping to ensure that investors and participants are aware of the possibility of investment losses and have clear information about TDF asset allocations. However, we found that DOL could take additional steps to better promote more careful and thorough plan sponsor selection of TDFs as default investments, and help plan participants understand the relevance of TDF assumptions about contributions and withdrawals.

ABBREVIATIONS

CIT	collective investment trust
DC	defined contribution
DOL	Department of Labor
EBSA	Employee Benefits Security Administration
ERISA	Employee Retirement Income Security Act
ICI	Investment Company Institute
IRA	individual retirement account
NAICS	North American Industry Classification System

OCC	Office of the Controller of the Currency
PPA	Pension Protection Act of 2006
QDIA	qualified default investment alternative
REIT	real estate investment trust
SEC	Securities and Exchange Commission
TDF	target date fund
TIPS	Treasury Inflation-Protected Security

* * *

January 31, 2011

The Honorable Herb Kohl
Chairman
Special Committee on Aging
United States Senate

The Honorable George Miller
Ranking Member
Committee on Education and the Workforce
House of Representatives

The financial security of millions of Americans in their retirement years will substantially depend on their savings in 401(k) and other defined contribution (DC) plans. To help ensure adequate financial resources for retirement, participants in DC plans must make adequate contributions during their working years and invest contributions in a way that will facilitate adequate investment returns over time. Typically, 401(k) plan sponsors have offered participants a menu of investment options in which they may invest account balances.

The Pension Protection Act of 2006 (PPA) included various provisions designed to encourage greater retirement savings among workers eligible to participate in 401(k) plans, such as provisions that facilitate plan sponsors' adoption of automatic enrollment policies.[1] Under such policies, eligible workers are automatically enrolled unless they explicitly decide to opt out of participation. Because an automatic enrollment program must also include a default investment—a vehicle in which contributions will be invested absent a specific choice by the plan participant—the act also directed the Department of Labor (DOL) to assist employers in selecting default investments that best serve the retirement needs of workers who do not direct their own investments. Since that time, target date funds (TDF)—that is, investment funds that invest in a mix of assets, and shift from higher-risk to lower-risk investments as a participant approaches their "target" retirement date—have emerged as by far the most popular default investment.

Nonetheless, TDFs have been the subject of considerable recent controversy. While TDFs are designed to decrease the risk of investment losses as a participant approaches the target date, some TDFs designed for those expecting to retire in 2010 experienced major losses during the financial market downturn of 2008-2009, placing the retirement security of many participants in jeopardy. Additionally, TDFs with the same target retirement year performed quite differently in recent years. In order to obtain more information about these and other developments, you asked us to examine a number of issues related to TDFs as qualified default investment alternatives (QDIA). Specifically, we addressed the following questions:

1. To what extent do the investment compositions of different TDFs vary?
2. What is known about the performance of TDFs?
3. How do plan sponsors select and monitor TDFs that are chosen as the plan's default investment, and what steps do they take to communicate information on these funds to their participants?
4. What steps have DOL and the Securities and Exchange Commission (SEC) taken to ensure that plan sponsors appropriately select and use TDFs?

To answer these questions, we conducted in-depth interviews with officials representing selected TDFs, plan sponsors, retirement plan consultants, DOL, SEC, and other experts. The eight TDF managers we contacted account for about 86 percent of the TDF market, as measured by assets under management. We also reviewed available documentation describing the asset allocation of selected TDFs, as well as the rationale behind these allocations. We obtained and summarized data regarding recent performance of various TDFs from Morningstar.[2] We also reviewed nine studies that, based on various techniques, projected a range of long- term investment outcomes for TDFs. We also reviewed federal laws and regulations.

We conducted our work from December 2009 to January 2011 in accordance with all sections of GAO's Quality Assurance Framework that are relevant to our objectives. The framework requires that we plan and perform the engagement to obtain sufficient and appropriate evidence to meet our stated objectives and to discuss any limitations in our work. We believe that the information and data obtained, and the analysis conducted, provide a reasonable basis for any findings and conclusions in this product.

BACKGROUND

Under DC plans, employees typically must decide whether or not to join the plan, as well as specify the size of their contributions and select one or more investments among the options offered by the plan. About 13 percent of the full-time workforce with access to employer-sponsored plans does not participate in such plans.[3] As GAO reported in 2009, existing studies have shown that automatically enrolling employees in 401(k) plans can substantially increase participation rates.[4] Among other things, automatic enrollment programs require plan sponsors to choose an investment that participants will be defaulted into if they do not make an election on their own. Historically, plan sponsors with such policies have used relatively conservative, low-return investments as the default investment because of fears of fiduciary liability from investment losses. However, the PPA included a number of provisions designed to encourage greater adoption of automatic enrollment, including limited protection from fiduciary liability for plans that automatically invest contributions in specific types of investments as defined by DOL. For example, in the absence of direction from an employee, plans that automatically invest contributions in such funds are treated as if the employee exercised control over management of their savings in the plan. As a result, fiduciaries of plans complying with DOL regulations have some protection against liability for losses that occur as a result of such investments. Fiduciaries—typically plan sponsors—must still satisfy the Employee Retirement Income Security Act (ERISA) fiduciary responsibilities when selecting and monitoring investment options available to plan participants, including QDIAs.[5] Specifically, plan sponsors who act as fiduciaries and other fiduciaries must act solely in the interest of plan participants and beneficiaries, in accordance with plan documents, act with prudence, and offer a diversified set of investment options with reasonable fees. After enactment of the PPA, DOL designated three types of QDIAs including the following:[6]

- **A product such as a TDF (also known as a life cycle fund):** A product that takes into account the individual's age or retirement date and invests in a mix of investments that become more conservative as the participant approaches his or her retirement date.
- **A product such as a balanced fund:** A product that takes into account the group of employees as a whole, instead of an individual, and that invests in a mix of assets with a level of risk appropriate for the group.
- **An investment service such as a professionally managed account:** Unlike a TDF, which is an investment *product*, a managed account is an investment *service* that typically allocates contributions among existing plan options so as to provide a mix of assets that takes into account an individual's age or retirement date and other circumstances.

Of the three options DOL identified, TDFs have quickly emerged as by far the most popular QDIA among plan sponsors who have automatic enrollment programs. As GAO reported in 2009, the percentage of Vanguard Group plans with TDFs as a default investment grew from 42 percent in 2005 to over 80 percent in 2009.[7] Pension industry experts we spoke with believed the popularity of TDFs will continue to grow in the future.

TDFs are a relatively new type of investment vehicle, and some large TDFs have less than 6 years of history. They are often established as mutual funds in a fund-of-funds structure. That is, the TDF is a composite of multiple underlying mutual funds in different asset classes. As figure 1 illustrates, TDFs consist of an equity component and a fixed income component.[8] The major asset classes, in turn, may be composed of funds representing different sectors of the major asset classes. For example, the equity component may consist of some funds focused on equities of large U.S. corporations, international equities, or equities of smaller companies. Similarly, the fixed income component may consist of various bond funds, such as funds consisting of government and corporate bonds.

A TDF can also be established in forms other than as a mutual fund. For example, TDFs may be offered as collective investment trusts (CIT), which are bank-administered pooled funds established exclusively for qualified plans such as 401(k)s. The responsible bank acts as the fiduciary, and holds legal title to the CIT assets. According to Morningstar, CITs offer a number of potential advantages over TDF mutual funds. For example, they feature lower costs because of factors such as reduced marketing expenses and fewer regulatory filings. Also, because they are not regulated as mutual funds, they can invest in certain vehicles that mutual funds cannot.

Also, some plan sponsors have established customized TDFs, instead of relying on preexisting TDFs offered by investment management firms. For example, a plan sponsor may develop a customized TDF using the existing core investment options it offers. Customized funds can be more precisely tailored to match a plan's objectives and demographics, and offer a plan sponsor greater control over the underlying investments of a TDF. However, one expert noted that because customized funds involve costs greater than those of an already-existing fund, they are generally more popular among larger plan sponsors.

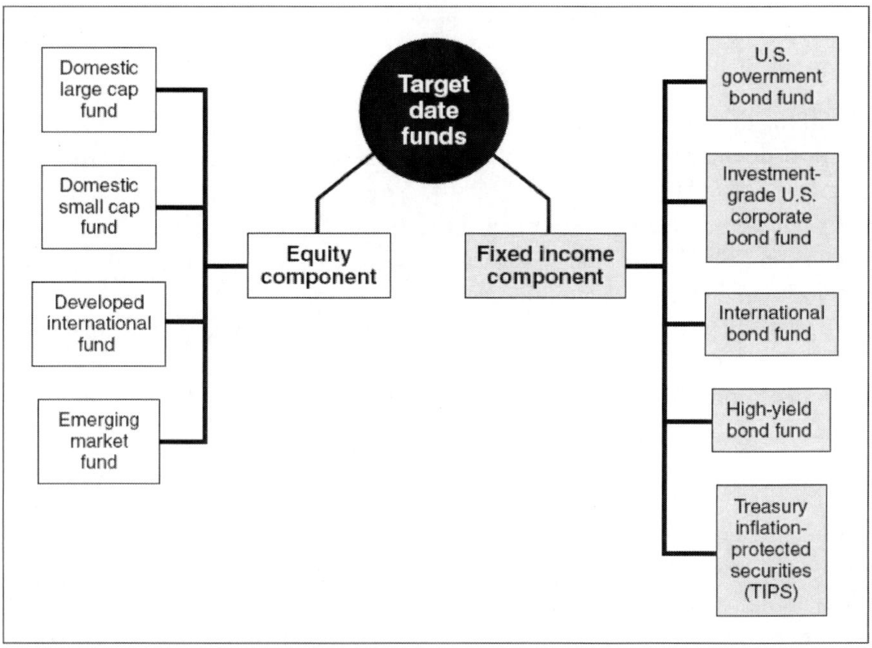

Source: GAO.

Note: This chart is for generic illustrative purposes only, and is not intended to illustrate the TDF of a particular investment firm. It is also not an exhaustive list of the asset types that may compose a TDF. For example, a TDF may also hold cash.

Figure 1. Example of a TDF's Fund-of-Funds Structure.

As a result of the controversies surrounding TDFs and at the request of Congress, DOL and SEC held a joint June 2009 hearing on TDFs. Among other issues, the agencies sought testimony regarding how TDF managers determine asset allocations, how they select and monitor underlying investments, and how such information is disclosed to investors. In October 2009, the U.S. Senate Special Committee on Aging held hearings on TDFs and issued a subsequent report.[11]

Investment Structures of TDFs Vary Considerably, and Their Design May Reflect Assumptions That Do Not Match Participant Behavior

TDF Allocations Vary Based on Different Objectives and Considerations

TDFs differ considerably in the degree to which they reduce allocation to equities in favor of fixed income investments approaching and after the target date. Each of the eight TDF managers included in our review allocated at least 80 percent of assets to equities 40 years before retirement. However, the rate at which the equity component is decreased and the size of the equity component at retirement can differ considerably. As figure 3 illustrates, one of the TDFs in our review has an equity allocation of about 65 percent at the target date, while another has an equity allocation of about 33 percent.[12]

In addition, some TDF glide paths reach their lowest equity allocation at the presumed retirement date, while others continue to reduce the equity allocation 10 or more years beyond the target date. In figure 3, for example, Fund B reaches its lowest allocation to equity—33 percent—at the target date, and this allocation is maintained for as long as the participant remains in the fund. In contrast, Fund A reaches the target date with an equity allocation of 65 percent, but the equity allocation continues decreasing for 15 years after the target date, ending at 35 percent.[13]

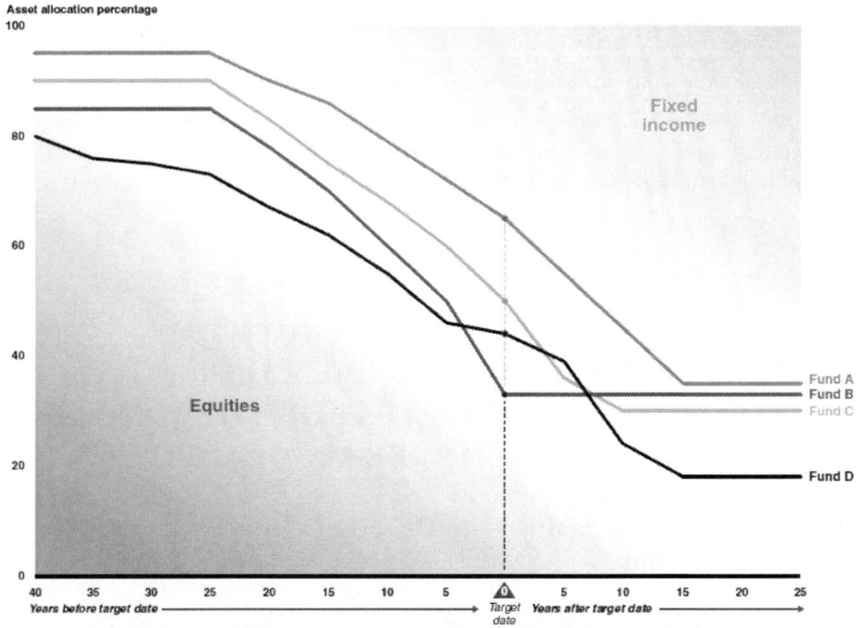

Source: GAO representation of data provided by selected TDF managers.

Note: One of these funds also includes commodities in the non-equity portion of its asset mix. This allocation declines from about 9.8 percent of total assets 40 years before the target date to about 2.0 percent 25 years after the target date.

Figure 3. Selected TDF Glide Paths.

Differences in the size of the equity component throughout the TDF's glide path may be rooted in different goals and in the treatment of various considerations such as the risk of losing money because of financial market fluctuations—investment risk—and the risk that a participant could outlive his or her assets—longevity risk. For example, two TDF managers whose funds had relatively high allocation to equity at the target date had TDFs designed to ensure that participants do not deplete their assets in retirement. One of these officials explained that even after retirement most participants need the growth that equities can provide and that overreliance on cash and bonds will not yield satisfactory results. According to analyses this manager performed, assuming that participants withdrew 5 percent of their initial savings each year, a strategy allocating 60 percent to equity and 40 percent to bonds would significantly reduce the risk that plan participants would deplete their assets during retirement, compared with a strategy of holding only bonds and cash.[14]

Another TDF manager with a relatively high equity allocation at the target date shared similar views, noting that the risk of a participant outliving retirement assets should be the key driver of managing retirement portfolios, and that the manager maintains a significant equity allocation to attain that objective. According to analyses this manager performed, a relatively high equity allocation better ensures that assets will last through a 30-year retirement than a lower equity alternative.

In contrast, TDF managers with significantly lower equity allocations throughout the fund's glide path cited other considerations. For example, the two TDF managers with relatively low allocations to equity at retirement we contacted stressed the potential volatility of equities and the importance of avoiding major losses to retirement savings near or after the target date. An official of one of these funds explained that the goal of the TDF is not to ensure that savings last through the retirement years, but to ensure that the maximum number of participants achieve a minimum acceptable level of savings *at* the retirement date. A representative of this TDF manager explained that while this glide path sacrifices the possibility of high investment returns for some participants, it is more important to ensure that as many people as possible arrive at the retirement date with an *adequate* level of savings. This is especially true for defaulted investors who may pay little attention to investment management, the official noted. As this official explained the manager's philosophy, the "pain" of arriving at retirement with insufficient savings outweighs the "pleasure" of arriving at retirement with more than is needed. The glide path of this TDF ends at the target date, and the TDF is not designed to manage assets in the retirement years. Instead, according to a representative of this TDF, it is assumed that participants will use accumulated savings to purchase an annuity at retirement. Similarly, a representative of another TDF said that a low equity allocation was chosen in order to lessen the possibility of severe, unrecoverable losses near retirement. An official of this TDF noted that the risk of investment losses at and after retirement is compounded by the fact that a participant is withdrawing money for living needs. The official noted that while a market loss of 10 percent during the working years can be made up by future contributions and market recovery, it may be difficult to recover from a loss of 10 percent at or just after retirement.

Our contacts with TDF managers revealed that TDFs are also designed based on certain key assumptions about participant actions that may not match what many participants actually do. For example, the glide paths of six of the eight TDFs we contacted extend beyond the target date, and thus seek to manage assets beyond the target date. However, some TDF managers and other experts indicated that this may be a faulty approach for many participants. For example, one TDF manager noted that its research revealed that of all workers who leave an employer after the age of 60, within 6 years, only about 20 percent are still invested in the plan. The official said that about 60 percent roll over into an individual retirement account (IRA), while 20 percent take a lump-sum distribution. A 2009 study of TDF asset allocations and participant behavior found that participants contribute less to their retirement accounts, and borrow and withdraw more, compared with common industry expectations.[15] This study noted that the average participant withdraws over 20 percent of his or her savings per year after retirement, and concluded that partly for this reason, designing a glide path that extends beyond the target date was undesirable. Other experts we contacted indicated that TDFs designed to manage savings in the retirement years may make a flawed assumption when they assume that participants will generally withdraw and spend savings in a methodical, sustainable manner. For example, a representative of a major retirement plan consulting firm stated that participants typically attempt to retain their previous lifestyle by drawing down assets more rapidly than is sound or than TDF managers generally assume.

Conversely, TDF managers who end the glide path at retirement may also be making assumptions that do not match participant actions. For example, representatives of one TDF manager who ends the glide path at retirement explained that the TDF is not designed to manage assets beyond retirement. Instead, the manager bases its income replacement calculations on the assumption that participants will cash out of the TDF upon retirement, and buy an annuity to provide retirement income. However, another TDF manager indicated that very few retirees buy an annuity. Other experts noted that it is not clear how TDF participants will manage withdrawals required for living needs. Further, because widespread adoption of automatic enrollment is a relatively new development, it is not known whether the withdrawal pattern of defaulted investors will differ from existing patterns.

TDFs are also designed based on certain assumptions about contribution rates that may not match what is known about prevailing contribution patterns, or the impact of default contribution rates. Each of the eight TDF managers we contacted considered contribution rates in establishing its asset allocation strategy, and some explicitly noted that these assumptions did not match the general pattern of contribution rates. For example, one noted that while contribution rates are generally lower than levels assumed by its model, it is hoped that rates will increase as workers adjust to DC plans serving as the sole employer-based retirement account. Another TDF manager noted that available data indicated that participant actions are much more varied and volatile than many TDF managers had assumed. According to this manager, participants generally start saving later and do not save at the rates generally assumed. Further, as we reported in 2009, participants who are automatically enrolled can be significantly influenced by the default contribution rate and default investment.[16] Specifically, we reported that studies had found that some workers would have selected a contribution rate higher than the default rate, had they enrolled in the plan voluntarily. These studies found that default mechanisms have this impact because the default requires no action on the part of the participant. Also some participants may see default policies as implicit advice from the plan sponsor. Because many participants are likely to be automatically enrolled in a TDF, given its emerging role as the predominant QDIA, the default contribution rate, as well as any automatic contribution escalation policy, could have a significant effect on contribution rates to TDFs.

Discussions with plan sponsors indicated that assumptions regarding participant saving and withdrawal patterns involve trade-offs. For example, several TDF managers told us that they had considered a range of contribution and postretirement withdrawal scenarios—to ensure that the TDF was suitable for a range of participants' saving and spending patterns. However, there may be drawbacks to designing TDFs in this manner. For example, one TDF manager noted that designing a TDF in this way could penalize participants who save and withdraw in a disciplined manner. This manager noted that the manager's TDF was designed with certain optimal assumptions in mind, and was not based on actual patterns of cash-out and postretirement spending behavior. The TDF manager explained that designing a TDF to ensure that an optimally behaving investor would not deplete his or her assets is a significant challenge in itself—it would be more difficult, and possibly counterproductive, to take into account actual investor behavior. Another TDF manager indicated that the TDF is designed with a higher equity allocation in the expectation that this will generate higher returns, and thereby, to some extent, compensate for low savings and high withdrawal rates of some participants. Some experts criticized this approach as taking excessive risks to make up for suboptimal participant behavior. For example, a representative of one major consulting firm noted that such an approach could make an underfunded retirement account run out of money even faster in the event of poor market returns.

TDFs' Investment Approaches Differ in Other Significant Aspects

While the differences in equity and fixed income allocations distinguish TDFs, these funds also vary in the content and management of these components.

Underlying Composition of Equity and Fixed Income Components

TDFs may vary in the allocations they make to different classes of equity, such as domestic and international. A representative of one TDF told us that the fund has a higher allocation to international equity than most other TDFs because fund managers expect returns in nondomestic markets to be higher in coming years, with little to no additional risk. TDFs can also take distinctly different approaches to selecting and managing their equity portfolios. While some TDF managers we contacted seek mainly to gain exposure to the general domestic or international equity funds, some TDF managers indicated that the manager invests in order to ensure exposure to different investment styles as well. For example, one TDF manager seeks to invest in equities through both "quantitative" and "fundamental" approaches.[17] According to this TDF manager, using both investment styles is intended to smooth the performance curve so that the equity component of the TDF will outperform the market in a smooth rather than erratic fashion.

The fixed income component of the TDFs we examined typically included both traditional fixed income investments, as well as newer vehicles such as high-yield bonds and Treasury Inflation-Protected Securities (TIPS).[18] Although high-yield bonds are generally much riskier than investment-grade bonds, some TDF managers told us they can serve as important diversifiers. One TDF manager said that the returns of high-yield fixed income investments tend to have an inverse relationship with investment-grade fixed income investments and thereby help smooth out the returns of the fixed income component. Nonetheless, because of their high risk, this TDF manager reduces the high-yield bond allocation as a participant nears the target date. Similarly, several TDF managers noted that TIPS are added to the fixed income component in the years before retirement. As one manager explained, the increase of fixed income securities later in the glide path results in greater exposure to inflation, and TIPS offer some inflation protection.

Passive versus Active Management

Most of the eight TDF managers we contacted rely on varying degrees of active management, generally in the belief that the returns of such actively managed funds will exceed those of general market indexes over time. For example, representatives of one TDF explained that they believed that the financial markets are not perfectly efficient, and that active management can outperform market indexes with only a modest degree of additional risk.[19] In contrast, one TDF manager and one plan sponsor with a customized fund said they are skeptical of active management, and rely primarily on passively managed funds, which seek to attain performance equal to market or index returns. According to an official of one manager, reliance on passively managed funds offers lower fees to investors. Partly for this reason, the official said that plan fiduciaries should opt for reliance on passive approaches because of their growing use as default investments. Further, such TDF managers expressed skepticism that active managers can persistently outperform the market over time.

Some TDFs rely on relatively unconstrained active management, using techniques similar to those used by some hedge funds. For example, one TDF manager we contacted uses some underlying funds based on absolute return strategies, which seek to achieve a positive total return that exceeds the rate of inflation by a targeted amount regardless of market conditions.[20] These absolute return funds have no fixed allocations and can shift assets from equities to fixed income or to other asset classes in a relatively unconstrained manner. Also, in an effort to achieve fund objectives, some of these funds use financial instruments such as options, futures contracts, and swaps.[21] This TDF manager allocates about 60 percent of TDF assets to absolute return funds at and after the retirement date.

Tactical Investment Allocation

Some TDFs permit tactical allocation—the use of short-term investment flexibility to depart from the stated investment strategy of the TDF—while other TDF managers opposed the use of such flexibility. Several TDF managers told us that they use tactical allocation in order to limit volatility and avoid large short-term investment losses, or to achieve greater long- term returns. For example, after the 2008-2009 market decline, one TDF manager adopted a tactical allocation policy with the aim of limiting volatility. Managers of this fund likened their tactical allocation to a shock absorber, and use a number of techniques—such as assessing trends in short-term and intermediate-term volatility and measuring correlations between asset classes—to assess the likelihood of oncoming financial market shocks. On the basis of these metrics, the fund may shift a portion of the equity allocation to fixed income assets if a decline in the equity market is foreseen. Another TDF manager noted that modest tactical asset allocation shifts over time can enhance fund performance, depending on the outlook in the financial markets. This fund will increase or reduce allocations to various asset classes and sectors by plus or minus 5 percent. Figure 4 illustrates an example of a tactical allocation policy—the middle band represents the degree of flexibility the fund manager has to deviate from the strategic equity allocation.

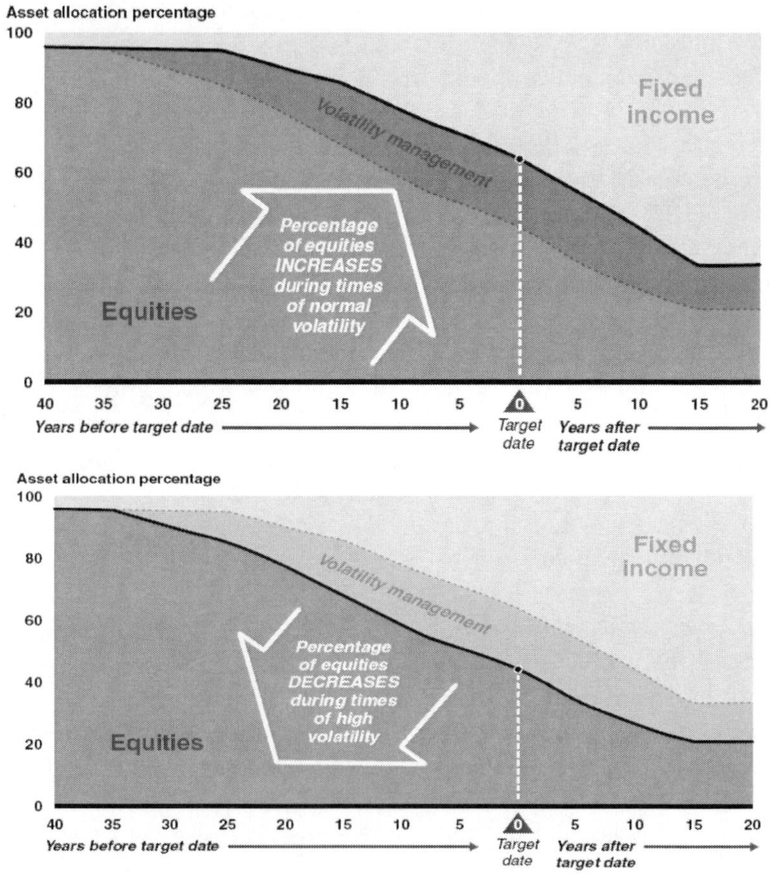

Source: GAO representation of example provided by a TDF manager.

Figure 4. Representation of TDF Glide Path with Tactical Allocation Option.

Three of the eight TDF managers we contacted do not use tactical allocation, preferring to rely on their long-term strategy. One TDF manager noted that severe market events such as the 2008-2009 decline can be likened to a 100-year flood, and that the possibility of such an event was considered in developing its TDF investment strategy. Representatives of these funds indicated that they had confidence in their long-term strategic allocation.

Use of Alternative Investments

Some of the TDFs in our study invested in alternative asset classes such as real estate investment trusts (REIT), other forms of real estate, or commodities.[22] TDFs that invest in alternative assets generally do so to limit volatility or to protect against the effects of inflation. For example, one TDF manager said that it invests in commodities as a form of inflation protection, but noted that because commodities are volatile, they are used earlier in the glide path, for younger workers. Similarly, another TDF manager said that it invests in REITs because they have some characteristics of fixed income investments and some equity-like characteristics, but have not historically correlated to either of these asset classes.

Some TDF managers we contacted who do not invest in such alternative investments expressed some skepticism about the benefits of such investments. For example, one TDF manager noted that nontraditional asset classes and complex investment strategies also come with greater risk and higher costs. For these reasons, the manager believes that such strategies do not offer a reasonable trade-off for the vast majority of retirement investors, especially for those defaulted into 401(k) investments.

Other Aspects of TDFs Can Affect Costs and Available Investments

The fees charged by TDFs vary in both structure and size. For TDFs composed of mutual funds, TDF fees are generally based on the costs of the underlying mutual funds, excluding sales loads and redemption fees. Some TDFs also apply an overlay fee representing the costs of establishing and managing the TDF. For example, one TDF manager explained that the firm does not charge an overlay fee because it believes greater revenues will be earned in the absence of such a fee, as the TDF attracts a greater volume of assets as a result. On the other hand, a TDF manager who did include an overlay fee stated that the effort involved in designing and managing the TDF itself justified imposition of a fee of about 3 basis points—that is, 0.03 percent. According to a 2010 industry analysis, asset-weighted expense ratios ranged from 0.19 percent to 1.71 percent.[23] In other words, the costs of the most expensive TDF in the analysis were about nine times the costs of the least expensive fund.

Some TDFs have a "closed" architecture in which underlying funds are limited to mutual funds operated by the firm offering the TDF, while other TDFs have an "open" architecture that may include both proprietary mutual funds and mutual funds managed by other firms. According to TDF managers and others, both types offer certain advantages and trade-offs. For example, some advocates of an open architecture asserted that this approach enables a TDF manager to select the best-performing underlying funds, regardless of who offers them. In addition, some have argued that open architecture removes a potential conflict of interest—the possibility that a TDF manager will invest in a new or poorly performing proprietary fund that is unable to attract sufficient investments on its own. On the other hand, a manager of a closed architecture TDF told us advocates of open architecture assume that there are fund managers who consistently outperform others. This TDF manager asserted that this is not the case. Further, the manager asserted that for some TDF managers, the TDF is or will become the flagship investment fund, and there would be little incentive for a manager to intentionally use a poorly performing fund as an underlying fund in the TDF. A 2010 study by Morningstar acknowledged the debate over open versus closed architecture, but noted that, based on its analysis, there was not a clear performance differential between open and closed architecture TDFs.[24]

TDFs Are Likely to Provide a Broad Range of Investment Returns

TDF investment returns have varied considerably in the last 5 years, from year to year as well as between similarly dated TDFs in a single year. Over the long term, studies that project TDF performance over a full working career reveal that different age cohorts may experience considerably different investment returns. Finally, comparisons of TDFs with different asset allocations and with other investment options such as balanced funds reveal a number of trade-offs.

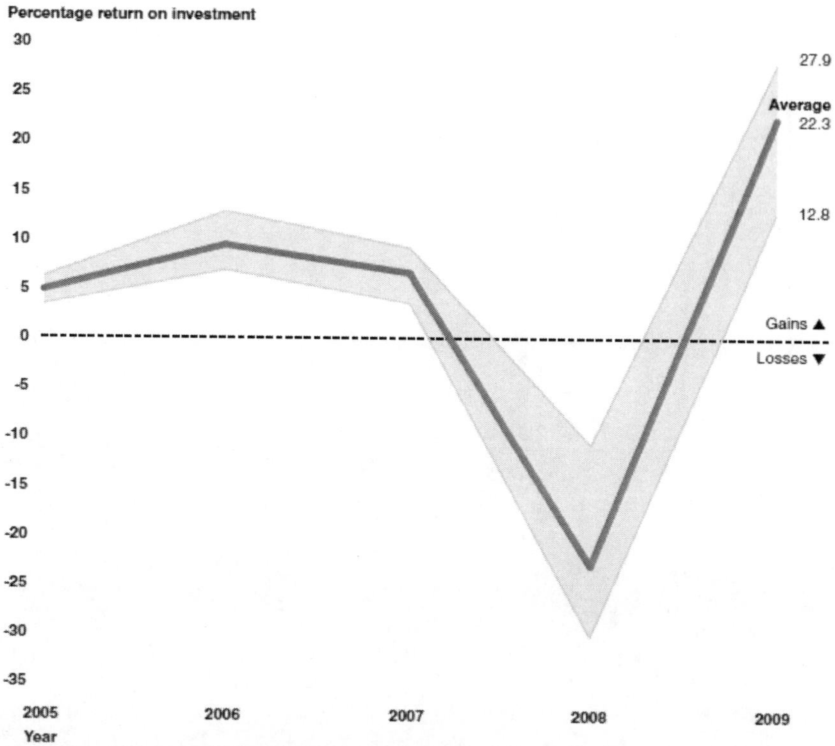

Source: GAO representation of Morningstar data.

Note: Morningstar provided data on the 15 largest 2010 TDFs in terms of assets under management, which represent 98 percent of the TDF market. For this representation, GAO selected the 8 funds that had at least 5 years' worth of return data available. Some TDFs are so new they do not have 5 years of return data. Furthermore, some TDFs contain multiple share classes. Returns from the subclass of shares with the most assets under management are represented.

Figure 5. Range of Returns from 2005 to 2009 for the 2010 TDFs with the Largest Market Share.

Performance for Similarly Dated TDFs Varied Over Recent Years

In recent years, year-to-year performance of TDFs of the same target date has varied considerably. As figure 5 illustrates, of the largest TDFs with 5 years of demonstrated returns, the returns have varied.

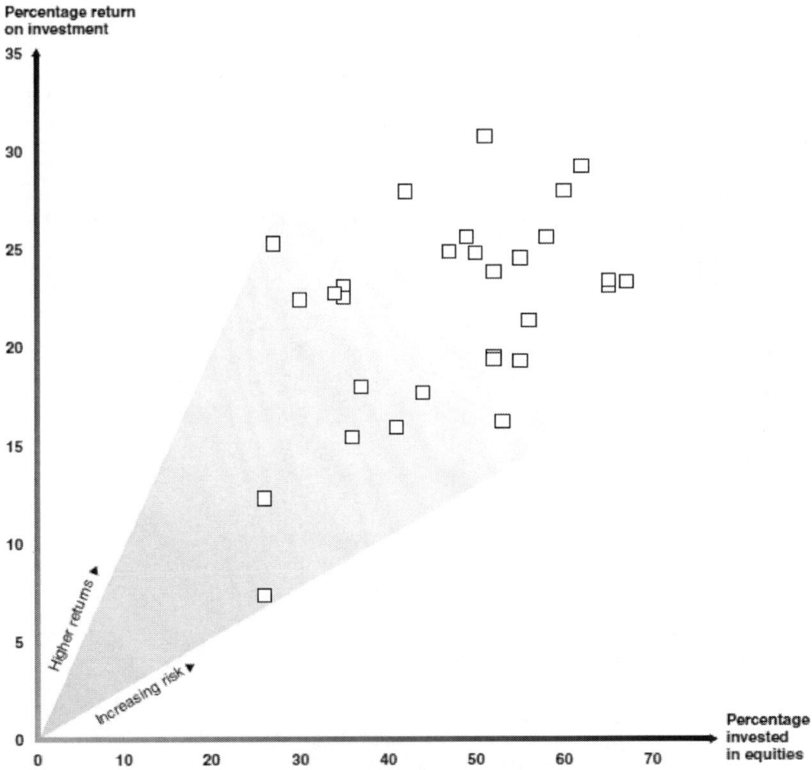

Source: GAO representation of Morningstar data.

Figure 6. 2010 TDF Returns in 2009 with Equity Allocation.

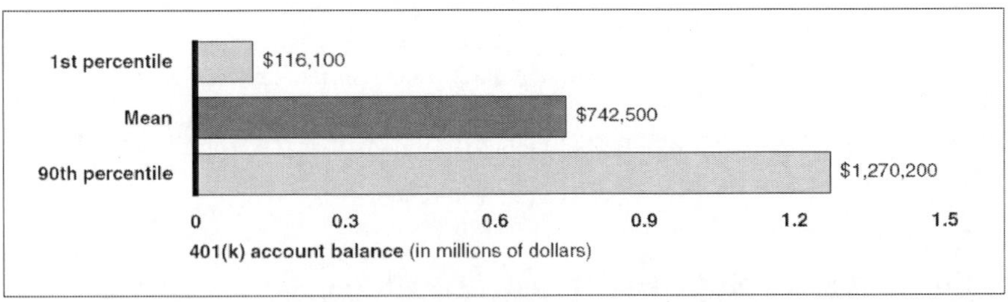

Source: GAO representation of J. Poterba, K. Rauh, S. Venti, and D. Wise. "Reducing Social Security PRA Risk at the Individual Level– Lifecycle Funds and No-Loss Strategies."

Figure 7. Potential Outcomes for TDF Ending Account Balances for College Graduates.

Investment returns also varied considerably between TDFs of the same target date within each year. For example, according to data from the 2009 Morningstar Industry Survey, in 2008, returns for 2010 TDFs ranged from a loss of about 41 percent to a loss of about 9 percent.[25] Conversely, with the market recovery in 2009, returns for 2010 TDFs ranged from gains of about 7 percent to gains of about 31 percent. Figure 6 illustrates 1 year of returns (2009) for 2010 TDFs along with the equity allocations of these TDFs, showing that there is a broad range of returns, even within 1 year, for similarly dated TDFs.

Because TDFs are designed to be long-term investments, short-term gains or losses need to be put into proper context; that is that these investments are expected to fluctuate in value over time. For example one expert we spoke to emphasized that the reported TDF returns in the last several years were based on the volatile economy. This volatility was not unique to TDFs but seen in varying degrees by other investments over that period of time.

Long-Term Performance of TDFs May Vary among Cohorts

The data from each of the nine studies included in our review showed that participants in different cohorts may experience different investment results.[26] For example, a 2006 study used historical earnings data and simulated asset returns to project ending account balances at the retirement date for (1) participants who began investing in different periods of their careers, and (2) participants of different educational levels.[27] As figure 7 illustrates, the study found that college graduates who experienced outcomes in the lowest percentile of returns could possibly accumulate savings of about $116,000, while the outcomes for those at the 90th percentile of returns could possibly accumulate about $1,270,000—or potentially more than 10 times the savings accumulated by the first percentile. The mean accumulation outcomes for college graduates were about $743,000. Similar ranges in potential outcomes were found for other educational groups.[28]

Another study found when completing simulations that while some participant cohorts might achieve greater returns than other participant cohorts, a small percentage of individual participants might arrive at retirement with less money in real terms than they contributed to their TDF over their working careers, because of poor returns in the financial markets.[29] Specifically, simulations completed in the study resulted in a mean real internal rate of return for the baseline portfolio of about 4.6 percent for all participant cohorts, while two simulated cohorts achieved a 2.4 percent real internal rate of return, or less than half the rate of return that the best-performing cohort achieved at 6 percent.[30] Furthermore, the study found that the mean rate of return for all individual participants was 4.3 percent, while individual participants in the 99th percentile achieved 8.5 percent rate of return and the bottom 10th percentile of individual participants experienced a rate of return of 1.9 percent, and those participants in the 1st, or lowest, percentile experienced a rate of return of minus 0.1 percent.[31]

STUDIES OF COHORT RISK

In this report, participant cohorts are groups of similarly aged participants whose length of working careers and retirement dates are similar. Because financial market returns will differ over the working lives of participants of different ages, even if all other factors such as contribution levels and investment portfolios remained constant, participants' cohorts are likely to experience significantly different investment returns. Therefore the participants may reach retirement with very different account balances. The risk of being in a cohort that experiences relatively low investment returns is sometimes referred to as cohort risk. It is important to note that while all TDF investors experience cohort risk, cohort risk is not unique to TDFs. All participants in DC retirement plans are exposed to this risk, because DC plans place investment risks solely on individual participants.

The studies we reviewed examined the potential results of cohort risk using various techniques and metrics, and are thus difficult to compare side by side. For example, some studies used historical data on market returns, while others used stochastic techniques, which involve running simulations of thousands of different economic paths to project potential outcomes. Also, the studies used different metrics such as the internal rate of return, account balances at retirement, or the probability of outliving one's assets.

Trade-offs of Different TDFs' Asset Allocations

Some of the studies we reviewed found that trade-offs exist between higher-equity and lower-equity TDFs. For example, one study found that TDFs using a higher-equity approach resulted in higher average returns relative to a more conservative, lower-equity TDF.[32] However, the study also found that higher-equity TDFs increased the chance for an infrequent poor outcome because of the increased risk these investments carry. By comparison, a lower-equity approach will increase the likelihood that the participant cohort will not lose as much money in a downturn in the market, but forgoes the potential for large returns in an upturn in the market. One study found that reducing the risk of extreme outcomes by switching to a lower-equity approach earlier in the glide path involved a heavy penalty in terms of forgone accumulation of wealth.[33] An additional study simulated the use of the TDFs in retirement and found that participants in lower-equity TDFs are subject to a higher shortfall risk— ranging between 14 percent and 22 percent.[34] However, TDFs with lower equity allocations may also help participants avoid extremely poor investment returns.[35]

Comparison of TDFs with Other Types of Investments

Some of the studies we reviewed analyzed the potential long-term performance of TDFs compared with other investments, such as balanced funds and all-bond funds.[36] In one study, the moderate TDF outperformed the balanced fund in three of the seven age cohorts examined, while the balanced fund performed better in the other four cohorts.[37] Further, this study found that the mean return of the aggressive TDF exceeded that of the balanced fund, while the balanced fund mean return exceeded those of the conservative and baseline TDFs.[38] Another study found a balanced fund to have similar average returns to a baseline TDF, but with a wider variance in returns.[39] The study also modeled a 50/50 balanced fund and found that the balance fund generally performed better than the simulated TDF used for comparison. For example, the study calculated the after-tax income in retirement for a college graduate earning $55,000 per year who had invested in a TDF versus in a 50/50 balanced fund. If the participant's TDF performed in the top or middle set of outcomes, then the 50/50 fund would outperform the simulated TDF. However, at the bottom 10 percent of possible outcomes, the TDF and 50/50 balanced fund performance would be similar, thereby making payouts from both types of funds at retirement almost the same.

The results of a study we reviewed that compared TDFs with an all-bond fund found that TDFs would outperform the all-bond fund. The study modeled conservative, moderate, and aggressive TDFs.[40] Assuming markets behave as they have historically, all three TDFs were projected to have higher average returns than the all-bond fund. The TDFs average return rate ranged from 3.9 to 5.1 percent, while the all-bond fund had an average return rate of 2.1 percent.

Plan Sponsors May Face Challenges Selecting and Monitoring TDFs and Communicating to Their Participants

Plan sponsors and industry experts we spoke to identified several key considerations in selecting and monitoring TDFs, such as ensuring the TDF fits with key characteristics of the workforce. Plan sponsors face a number of challenges in selecting and monitoring TDFs, and some may not take a thorough approach to TDF selection. Although plan sponsors communicate to participants using different media, plan sponsors and others we contacted indicated that the level of understanding of TDFs among plan participants was fairly low, particularly among defaulted participants.

According to Plan Sponsors and Industry Experts, Plans Should Take Several Steps When Selecting and Monitoring TDFs as QDIAs

Clearly Defined Goals and Objectives

Plan sponsors and other experts we contacted noted that the unique and complex nature of TDFs necessitates certain steps in the selection and monitoring processes, above and beyond the steps plan sponsors would take for any 401(k) investment.[41] As one expert noted, TDFs are structured as a long-term, all-in-one investment solution, rather than a single investment product within a broader retirement portfolio. Several plan sponsors and others stated that plan sponsors should first clearly define their goals and objectives for the 401(k) plan's default investment and then choose TDFs that match these objectives. For example, if the goal of the 401(k) plan is to serve as the sole retirement vehicle for most participants, then a plan sponsor may wish to consider more conservative TDFs as its default investment. Conversely, if the goal of a 401(k) plan is to serve as a supplementary savings vehicle to accompany a defined benefit plan, a more aggressive TDF may be appropriate.

Matching TDF to Participant Population

Several plan sponsors and industry experts noted that each plan sponsor's participant population has certain characteristics that should be taken into account when determining which TDF to select as a default investment. For example, one plan sponsor said that its employees generally share similar relevant characteristics—most of its participants will retire before 65 years of age, have access to a defined benefit plan, maintain a reasonable savings rate, and receive 401(k) employer match in company stock. Therefore, the sponsor chose to develop its own customized TDF that would better match its workforce, rather than an off-the-shelf product. Several industry experts noted that a plan sponsor's industry, particularly the salary level and job security or turnover, should be considered when deciding which TDF to choose as the plan's default investment. For example, one expert noted that a glide path with a lower equity allocation would better suit a sponsor with a high-turnover workforce. This is because a participant would be less likely to suffer significant investment losses if he or she were to separate and cash out his or her 401(k) in a depressed equity market. While some plan sponsors and plan consultants may examine the participant population, small plan sponsors with unique and homogeneous workforces may benefit from simply identifying several key characteristics of their participant population and using that insight to inform their choice of TDFs as their default investment.

Similarly, some plan sponsors and others noted that plan sponsors should make an effort to match the TDF glide path and underlying assumptions with other workforce characteristics. In particular, industry experts and plan sponsors cited the importance of considering participants' behavior as it pertains to contribution rates, retirement age, withdrawal patterns during a participant's working career, and actions in retirement, such as drawdown rates.[42] Little is currently known about participants defaulted into TDFs, because they are relatively new vehicles that only recently have gained popularity as default investments. Consequently, many plan sponsors we spoke with examined their entire participant population to inform their TDF selection process. Similarly, given that QDIAs themselves are relatively new, it is unclear what the behavior of the defaulted population will be over time. Industry experts said that in some cases, a large majority of participants may take a lump-sum withdrawal at retirement, purchase an annuity, or reinvest the balance in a vehicle that the sponsor knows little about. In that case, according to one industry expert, a plan sponsor may wish to consider a TDF that reduces its market risk as the fund nears the retirement date because participants will be taking money out of their TDFs at retirement. In contrast, if most plan participants are going to withdraw funds from the plan at a steady rate throughout retirement, then a plan sponsor may wish to consider a TDF with a more aggressive glide path near the retirement date because the participant would have a longer time to recover from any downturns in the equity market. Furthermore, one industry expert said plan sponsors should examine participant contribution rates and withdrawal patterns, especially the percentage of participants who take preretirement distributions starting at 59½ years old. According to this expert, such distributions could substantially affect the volatility of cash flows and the investment time horizon for the TDF.

Despite the importance placed on workforce characteristics by some of the plan sponsors and experts we contacted, current DOL regulations do not require that plan fiduciaries, such as plan sponsors, consider factors other than a participant's age or target retirement date when deciding whether a TDF, among categories of investment alternatives described in the regulation, are QDIAs within the meaning of the regulation. While the current regulations do not preclude consideration of other factors, DOL has specifically stated that plan fiduciaries are not required to include other considerations in their selection of QDIAs. In the preamble accompanying the final QDIA regulations in 2007, DOL stated that the agency took this position in order to provide plan fiduciaries with certainty that they had complied with the regulation.[43] However, as mentioned in the preamble, plan fiduciaries still must satisfy their general fiduciary responsibilities of prudence and loyalty when selecting and monitoring any particular TDF, and these duties require plan fiduciaries to consider other factors in selecting a particular TDF.

Plan Sponsor Expertise and Resources

Because some TDFs are more challenging to monitor than others, some industry experts said plan sponsors should consider their level of expertise and available resources when selecting TDFs. Plan sponsors and industry experts stressed the importance of monitoring and assessing any changes to the TDF glide path or investment strategy because TDFs are not static investments. A TDF may deviate from or change its stated glide path over time, change underlying funds and fund managers, or change investment strategies within an asset class—all of which can have a significant effect on the fund's composition, performance, and fees. Therefore, as one industry expert stated, plan sponsors with limited expertise and resources should not select TDFs with high tactical allocations or other actively managed strategies that allow the TDF manager to deviate significantly from its glide path because they require more active oversight. Similarly, one industry expert said plan sponsors whose investment committees meet only once annually and rely primarily on their record keepers' reports to monitor their investments should not choose TDFs that would require more due diligence monitoring, such as customized funds.

Some Plan Sponsors Face Challenges When Selecting and Monitoring TDFs

Limited due Diligence

Our discussions with plan sponsors and industry experts indicated that sponsors vary in their approach to TDF selection and monitoring, in part because of several key challenges that some plan sponsors face. First, some plan sponsors, particularly small plan sponsors, who spend the vast majority of their time running their business and administering other benefits and payroll, may have limited resources in-house to conduct a thorough TDF selection process and ongoing monitoring activities. One industry expert noted that this may be a problem, particularly in the small end of the marketplace, where plan sponsors may simply choose any TDF in the marketplace once they determine that all TDFs qualify as QDIAs. Another industry expert stated that most plan sponsors could not even document that they had considered a range of investment managers in their TDF selection process.[44] Furthermore, some small plan sponsors may not grasp the basic concepts of TDFs and would not know the steps necessary to properly evaluate and select a TDF. Therefore, some plan sponsors with limited in-house resources may look outside to service providers for advice or to conduct some or all of the steps of the TDF selection and monitoring processes; however, they may be unaware that the service provider may not be a plan fiduciary and may have conflicts of interest in providing advice.[45]

Benchmarking Limitations

The majority of experts and plan sponsors we spoke to said that plan sponsors have difficulty comparing and evaluating the performance of TDFs because of the limitations of currently available benchmarks. According to several experts, traditional benchmarks, such as Morningstar star ratings, that compare the returns of all funds within a category—such as all domestic large cap funds—relative to each other, may not be very useful in evaluating TDF performance. This is because the objectives, asset allocation, investment strategy, and underlying funds that make up a TDF can vary among one another and over time. For example, a TDF with a relatively low allocation to equity may underperform a TDF benchmark during a lengthy rise in the equity market, but this may be an expected short-term consequence of the long-term TDF strategy. If a sustained decline in equity values occurs near or after the target date, the same TDF may outperform the benchmark. One plan sponsor pointed out that TDFs are a relatively new product type and most of them do not have long track records, yet these vehicles have long-term investment objectives (e.g., 40 years at a minimum and much longer if the postretirement phase is included.) Therefore, experts noted that simply comparing returns over a 1-, 5-, or 10-year time period might not be useful in evaluating the long-term appropriateness of the fund.

Some plan sponsors said they developed custom composite benchmarks to evaluate the performance of their individual TDFs. Other industry experts noted that custom composite benchmarks are useful only in measuring whether a manager succeeds in outperforming the general market but that they lack the ability to evaluate a TDF's glide path strategy or investment objectives. Several industry experts and plan sponsors we spoke to said there is no universally accepted benchmark that can be used to evaluate all TDFs. As an alternative to benchmarks, one plan consultant recommended that sponsors use forward-looking metrics that evaluate the risk/reward characteristics and the range of possible long-term performance outcomes of the TDFs—such as retirement income replacement rates and longevity risk (e.g., the risk that a participant will run out of money before death) as alternative evaluation tools.[46] Several plan consultants said plan sponsors would be best served to examine the fund's glide path and objectives, rather than focus solely on performance.

Role of Record Keepers

Several industry experts we spoke to said record keepers may influence a plan sponsor's TDF selection process.[47] Several industry experts said some record keepers require plan sponsors to use their TDFs or may offer discounts to entice plan sponsors to use their TDFs. Since the costs and time associated with switching a record keeper can be high—for example, this could entail changes in computer systems, record-keeping and payroll processes, and converting account balances—plan sponsors may feel they have little choice and may not even consider other options. According to Brightscope data, in 2009, 96 percent of 401(k) plans with TDFs that were clients of the largest record keepers use the record keeper's proprietary TDFs.[48]

Two of the 10 plan sponsors we spoke to said they did not look beyond their record keeper's TDFs when selecting their plan's default investment.

One said it chose not to search for other TDFs in the marketplace because it valued the bundled services approach that its record keeper could provide. This sponsor added that this arrangement made it easy for the plan sponsor to manage the 401(k) plan because it interacts with one provider for most issues it encounters. Another plan sponsor said it used an outside consultant to

conduct its TDF search. However, the first step in the consultant's search process was to get a list of funds that were supported by its record keeper. Ultimately, the consultant provided only one recommendation—the record keeper's TDF—to the plan sponsor's investment committee.

Plan Sponsors Provide Defaulted Participants Information on TDFs Using Various Media

Although most plan sponsors we spoke to offered multiple avenues of communications to their participants, the level of information on TDFs provided to plan participants varied greatly from plan sponsor to plan sponsor. Plan sponsors we spoke to provided information to participants on all 401(k) investments using a variety of media, which included new employee packets, flyers, newsletters, Web sites, call centers, and in- person educational sessions. In addition, some plan sponsors provided communications specifically focused on TDFs. For example, one plan sponsor sent a newsletter to participants after the 2008 market downturn that included an article explaining how TDFs should be used. Another sponsor said it provided a Morningstar fund fact sheet on all its 401(k) investments, including TDFs, and the initial and annual QDIA notifications, and provided no further information on TDF investing in general, or the composition of the TDFs offered in the 401(k) plan. In contrast, another plan sponsor said its employee benefits staff meets with new employees to review the TDF's glide path, discuss the age-based nature of the TDFs, and the importance of choosing a TDF with a target date closest to their planned retirement date. They also explained the risks and return characteristics of the TDFs and how they become more conservative over time. New employees also received a packet that included information on the available TDFs. Some plan sponsors relied on service providers to develop and distribute information on TDFs to their participants. One plan sponsor we spoke to said that all participant communications come directly from its record keeper and TDF manager.

Several plan sponsors said they sent initial and annual notifications directly to defaulted participants explaining that participants have been automatically enrolled in the 401(k) plan and defaulted into a specific TDF. However, defaulted participants may receive limited or no information on the principles and objectives of TDF investing, in general, or specific information on the glide path and composition of the TDFs chosen as the plan's default investment. If this information is not included in the annual communications sent to defaulted participants, then participants must actively seek out information on the TDFs they are invested in through other media, such as Web sites, educational tools and videos, and newsletters.

Plan sponsors and other experts described a number of challenges in effectively educating participants about key aspects of TDFs. Plan sponsors generally indicated that participants understand little about TDFs beyond the basic concept that TDFs are aged-based funds that become more conservative over time. The sponsors also indicated that participants defaulted into TDFs know less about TDFs than an average participant. One consultant said that defaulted participants are typically disengaged and, in general, could not name the fund that their contributions are going into or answer the most fundamental questions about TDFs. Furthermore, several plan sponsors we spoke to said that participants had misperceptions about TDFs, particularly those contributing to TDFs with target dates in the relatively near future. Such participants often believed that their investments were protected because they were close to the retirement date, and were shocked when the values declined significantly, as they did in 2008-2009.

Federal Agencies Have Taken Actions to Address Issues Related to TDFs

Since DOL and SEC held a hearing regarding TDFs in the wake of the 2008-2009 market decline, the agencies have taken several steps to enhance participant protections. These included efforts that focused on educating plan sponsors and participants, and proposed regulations that, if finalized, would require TDF managers and plan sponsors to improve information provided to participants.

Guidance on Selecting and Monitoring TDFs

In early 2010, DOL and SEC jointly published an investor bulletin that provided participants education and outlined considerations for plan participants when choosing a TDF.[49] The investor bulletin explained the goals, functions, and risks associated with TDFs while directing participants to carefully consider whether TDFs are the best option for them. The investor bulletin also explained that TDFs are designed to make investing for retirement more convenient by automatically changing the asset allocation for the participant's account over time. DOL and SEC emphasized that TDFs carry risk and do not guarantee sufficient retirement income at the retirement date. Because defaulted participants have not generally taken an active role in their investments, some experts expressed doubt that the bulletin would be of value to these participants.

According to DOL officials, the agency is also developing guidance directed at plan sponsors. DOL stated that the guidance was necessitated by the growing popularity of TDFs in 401(k)-type plans and the fact that TDFs are not uniformly designed investment products. According to DOL, the guidance will be designed to assist plan sponsors in their evaluation and selection of TDFs as plan investments, aiming to help plan fiduciaries enhance retirement security for participants. DOL noted that such guidance is needed in light of the importance of understanding the unique characteristics that distinguish TDFs from other types of investments, the differences among the various TDFs available, and how these differences can affect the retirement savings of participants. As of January 24, 2011, the guidance had not been released.

Actions to Enhance TDF Disclosure to Participants by Plan Sponsors

In recent months, both DOL and SEC have issued proposed regulations that would help ensure that plan participants obtain better information about TDFs. SEC proposed regulations addressing the marketing and naming of TDFs in June 2010.[50] According to the preamble of SEC's proposal, the proposed regulations are intended to address concerns that have been raised regarding the potential for investor misunderstanding that could arise from TDF names and marketing materials. In November 2010, DOL released proposed regulations on target date disclosures.[51] According to DOL officials, their proposal was largely motivated by the joint public hearing held by DOL and SEC in June 2009, after which the agency determined that improvements could be made to the information disclosed to participants concerning their investments in TDFs. SEC and DOL proposed regulations that are summarized in table 1.

Table 1. Recent SEC and DOL Regulatory Proposals for TDF Disclosure Requirements

SEC-proposed regulations for TDF marketing materials	DOL-proposed amendments to QDIA and other disclosure regulations for TDFs[a]
Prohibiting potentially misleading statements about TDFs	
Certain statements would be considered potentially misleading[b] • stating that TDFs are a "simple" investment plan that requires little or no monitoring by the participant, or • emphasizing a single factor, such as an investor's age, as the basis for determining that an investment is appropriate.	Not applicablec
Inclusion of general advisory statements	
Advertisements would be required to advise participants that • factors in addition to age or retirement date should be considered by investors, and that the loss of • the TDF investment is not guaranteed and money is possible including at and after the target date.	With regard to TDFs, fiduciaries must provide • a statement that participants may lose money by investing in a QDIA, including losses near or following retirement, and that there is no guarantee that investment in the QDIA will provide adequate retirement income.
Disclosure of specific information about TDFs	
Advertisements would be required to disclose information such as • TDFs that use the target date in the fund name must disclose asset allocation as of that date, immediately adjacent to the first use of the fund name; • a table, chart, or graph that illustrates asset allocation over the life of the TDF; • an explanation of the asset allocation changes over time, when the TDF will reach its final allocation, and a description of the final asset allocation; and	For all QDIAs: • basic information such as name of the investment issuer, • objectives and goals, • principal strategies and risks, • historical performance, and • information on plan fees. Specifically for TDFs: • asset allocation at the retirement/target date; • a table, chart, or graph that illustrates the TDF asset allocation over time;

SEC-proposed regulations for TDF marketing materials	DOL-proposed amendments to QDIA and other disclosure regulations for TDFs[a]
• whether asset allocations can be changed without shareholder vote.	• an explanation that the asset allocation changes over time and a description of the final asset allocation; • an explanation of the age group for whom the fund is designed, and the relevance of the target date; and • any assumptions made about a participant's contribution and • withdrawal intentions on or after the target date.

Source: GAO summary of SEC and DOL proposed regulations.

[a]The proposed DOL requirements specific to TDFs would apply to both participants invested in a QDIA by default and to those who actively choose to invest in a TDF.

[b]While TDFs are the immediate impetus for the proposed amendments, the proposed amendments would apply to all types of investment companies.

[c]Although DOL's proposed regulations do not address this issue, in its notice of proposed rulemaking, DOL requested comments as to whether and to what extent its final rule should include elements or concepts contained in SEC's rulemaking.

As table 1 shows, the regulations proposed by DOL and SEC contain some similar provisions that, if finalized, would help ensure that both plan participants and investors generally obtain more accurate information about TDFs. However, there are also some differences in the two agencies' proposed regulations, and the variations in these regulatory approaches are likely a reflection of the fact that each agency has its own purpose and its own authorities and responsibilities. For example, the DOL proposal would require that plan participants receive information on the assumptions about a participant's contributions and withdrawal intentions, which may be especially important for participants relying on a TDF as their main retirement savings vehicle.

SEC received 51 comments on its proposed regulation, and several commenters noted that additional disclosures might have very little impact on a large portion of TDF investors—specifically those who are and will be defaulted into the TDFs. For example, one commenter noted that many defaulted participants may have minimal interest in investing their account assets themselves. Further, the commenter noted that such participants are likely to remain in the default investment throughout their employment with the plan sponsor. Therefore, this commenter said it is especially important for plan sponsors to select an appropriate TDF on behalf of all defaulted participants. On the other hand, two commenters said SEC's proposed amendments could help defaulted participants to better understand the TDF's investment strategy and asset allocation plan, especially if these defaulted participants later choose to become more active investors.

Other Organizations Have Made Alternative Proposals Regarding TDF Regulation

In recent years, industry organizations and others have offered alternative perspectives that could be considered by DOL and SEC as they proceed with their regulatory and guidance efforts.

In June 2009, the Investment Company Institute (ICI), a mutual fund trade organization, published a set of principles aimed at improving disclosures by TDF managers.[52] For example, the document recommended that TDFs prominently disclose the fund's assumptions about the participants' withdrawal rates at and after the target date, and offered sample language that TDF managers might use. It noted that this information is important because a TDF's asset allocation can vary significantly approaching and after the target date based on such withdrawal assumptions. Also, it noted the importance of illustrating the assumptions that influenced the development of the glide path, and the possibility of glide path adjustments, such as a change in the strategic allocation to equities. The principles also stated that the relevance of the target date used in the fund name should be prominently disclosed. For example, the principles noted that such disclosure might prominently state that the fund name refers to the approximate year a participant would plan to retire and stop making contributions to the TDF. Furthermore, if the target date is also the date at which the participant is expected to cash out of the fund, this information could be disclosed as well.

Both ICI and AARP have also offered lists of issues that plan sponsors should consider in selecting TDFs.[53] ICI noted several considerations concerning plan participant characteristics, such as whether participants also have access to other retirement benefits, like a defined benefit plan, that plan sponsors should consider when choosing a TDF. AARP suggested that plan sponsors consider plan demographics such as workforce age and participant contribution rates. AARP also proposed that plan sponsors consider the TDF manager's investment objectives and assumptions used for determining these investment strategies and asset allocations. According to AARP, these could include assumptions about contribution and withdrawal rates, retirement horizon, and income needed in retirement.

CONCLUSION

TDFs are relatively new investments and have gained considerable popularity among plan sponsors as default investments only over the last several years. They are a significant development in the financial services and retirement plan industry, and may become the most common investment option in DC plans in the years ahead. Along with the growth of automatic enrollment policies, TDFs as QDIAs help "automate" certain aspects of DC plan participation that have been left to the discretion of plan participants in DC plans. However, TDFs do not address some of the other limitations of the DC plan system. For example, as with any other DC plan, plan participants contributing to TDFs still bear the full burden of investment risk. While studies have shown that many TDF investors are likely to do well, some percentage of participants may realize relatively poor real returns on their investments over their working life.

Further, plan sponsors and others have indicated that the process of selecting TDFs as default investments for 401(k) plans can vary considerably from one plan sponsor to another. To some degree, differences among plan sponsors are inevitable, because larger plan sponsors will generally have the resources to do more planning and research than smaller plan sponsors. However, the responsibilities of a plan sponsor to thoughtfully select and monitor TDFs are all the more important when participants are automatically enrolled and defaulted into the investment chosen by the plan sponsor. While plan sponsors and others we spoke to identified important steps, we found that there are also opportunities to help improve plan sponsor selection of TDFs. Developing guidance and tools could help to improve plan sponsor awareness of the key aspects and differences of TDFs in the marketplace. For example, some plan sponsors may place unwarranted reliance on TDF benchmarks, a practice that may be misleading given the long-term nature and different asset allocation strategies of TDFs. Information about the limitations of these benchmarks could help plan sponsors improve their approach to TDF selection. In addition, some plan sponsors and industry experts stressed the importance of considering workforce characteristics beyond age or retirement date in selecting a TDF. Such characteristics could include the existence of a defined benefit plan, salary level, turnover rate, or participant behavioral characteristics, such as contribution rates and withdrawal patterns.

We commend SEC and DOL for their ongoing efforts to help ensure that plan sponsors and participants select and use TDFs appropriately. In light of the recent emergence of TDFs as a typical default investment, we acknowledge some additional actions may best be taken after more is learned about how default investors use TDFs over the longer term. However, in the interim, DOL could take some additional steps. For example, it is important to note that some participants may not grasp the asset allocations of their TDF and the investment theories on which the allocations are based. This is especially likely for many of the participants who, given the overwhelming popularity of TDFs as QDIAs, will be defaulted into a TDF and may take a passive approach to their retirement savings. With minimal effort, defaulted participants who may have little interest in investments or the TDF asset allocation strategies could benefit from short, simple educational information about key assumptions that TDF managers make about plan participant actions. Accordingly, DOL's proposed amendments to the QDIA regulation include a requirement that plan sponsors provide any assumptions made about participants' contribution and withdrawal intentions on or after the target date to plan participants. However, it is not obvious from the proposed regulation that plan participants would receive information clearly explaining the potential connections among the assumptions made about participant contributions and withdrawals, the participants' related actions, and their ability to establish and sustain a financially secure retirement.

The current QDIA regulations do not require that plan sponsors consider workforce characteristics beyond a participant's age or retirement date in selecting TDFs as default investments, and the proposed regulatory amendments do not address this issue. As DOL explained when issuing the final QDIA regulations, consideration of other workforce characteristics, apart from age or retirement date, was not required in deciding whether TDFs, among the categories of investment alternatives described in the regulation, are QDIAs within the meaning of the regulation. This is because DOL wanted to give plan sponsors certainty that they had complied with the regulations. We agree that such certainty has value. However, much has been learned about TDFs in the years since the initial regulation was developed. In particular, it is clear that TDFs' asset allocations differ considerably, that these differences reflect different trade-offs regarding key risks, and that specific TDFs may therefore be well suited to the workforce characteristics of some plan sponsors, but not those of others. In satisfying their fiduciary obligations of prudence and loyalty in the selecting and monitoring of particular TDFs as QDIAs, plan fiduciaries may need to be aware of these differences.

RECOMMENDATIONS FOR EXECUTIVE ACTION

We recommend that the Secretary of Labor direct the Assistant Secretary of the Employee Benefits Security Administration to

1. amend the QDIA regulations so that fiduciaries are required to document that they have considered, to the extent possible, whether other characteristics of plan participants, in addition to age or target retirement date, are relevant factors in choosing a QDIA;
2. provide guidance to plan sponsors regarding the limitations of existing TDF benchmarks and the importance of considering the long- term TDF investment allocations and assumptions used in developing the TDF asset allocation strategy; and
3. in its final regulation on target date disclosure, expand the requirement that plan sponsors provide information regarding key assumptions concerning contribution and withdrawal rates by requiring that participants receive a statement regarding the potential consequences of saving, withdrawing, or otherwise managing TDF assets in a way that differs from the assumptions on which the TDF is based.

AGENCY COMMENTS

We provided a draft of this report to the Department of Labor, the Department of the Treasury, and the Securities and Exchange Commission for review and comment. The Department of Labor noted that the report accurately highlighted many of the structural and disclosure issues surrounding TDFs, and the challenges that face plan fiduciaries in selecting TDFs. However, DOL did not agree with our first recommendation, which called for it to require that plan fiduciaries, to the extent possible, consider characteristics of plan participants, other than age or retirement date, when choosing a QDIA. Labor reiterated, as we noted in our report, that it had considered and rejected this approach in developing the final QDIA regulations. DOL further stated that it is not clear whether GAO intended that fiduciaries consider some or all of the characteristics GAO mentioned, or how a fiduciary should interpret or apply such characteristics in selecting a TDF. DOL agreed, however, that it may be appropriate for a fiduciary to consider the characteristics that GAO cited, and indicated that the agency will include such considerations in its guidance to plan fiduciaries.

We stand by our recommendation. A great deal has been learned about TDFs since DOL developed its QDIA regulations. As we noted in our report, the asset allocations, risk levels, and assumptions concerning participant disposition of assets at and after the retirement date differ considerably among TDFs. Most recently, as the events of 2008 showed, these differences can have considerable impact on plan participants who are near retirement and thus particularly vulnerable to large investment losses. In light of this, we believe that a consideration of other participant characteristics in the QDIA selection process, to the extent that such information is available to a fiduciary, would better protect plan participants. We agree that it is important for fiduciaries to be certain that they have complied with all applicable regulations, but we believe that our recommendation would not add undue uncertainty or unnecessary complications to the QDIA selection process. Indeed, highlighting the importance of other workforce characteristics, as DOL proposes to do, without amending the QDIA regulations could cause more uncertainty regarding fiduciary obligations. However, in light of DOL's concerns, we have amended our recommendation so that it calls for DOL to require that plan sponsors consider whether other workforce characteristics are relevant, and document that they have done so. Combined with the guidance that DOL is developing, such a requirement would at least cause a plan fiduciary to consider whether a particular TDF is a reasonable fit for its workforce. As DOL noted in the QDIA regulation, consideration of other characteristics would be permissible but not required.

DOL indicated that it would consider our other two recommendations in the course of its ongoing regulatory and guidance efforts. We understand that DOL would not wish to take a position while its efforts are ongoing. However, we believe that the timing of our recommendation is particularly apt in light of these efforts, and we are hopeful that our work will inform DOL as it works to finalize the regulations.

DOL cited a number of concerns with our third recommendation, which called for the agency to require sponsors to provide information on the potential consequences of saving, withdrawing, or otherwise managing their

TDF assets in a way that differs from the assumptions on which a TDF is based. Specifically, DOL said that this would be a very complicated and subjective undertaking, which could affect a plan sponsor's decision to offer a TDF. We disagree. The Department of Labor already proposes to require sponsors to provide information about a TDF's assumptions concerning participants' contribution and withdrawal intentions. Our recommendation seeks to ensure that plan participants understand the significance of these assumptions. An additional statement of the kind we advocate could simply point out to plan participants that contributing at a rate lower than or withdrawing at a rate higher than a TDF's design assumptions could lessen the likelihood of a secure retirement.

We did not receive formal comments from the Department of the Treasury or the Securities and Exchange Commission, and received technical comments from the three agencies, which we incorporated as appropriate.

Charles A. Jeszeck
Director, Education, Workforce,
and Income Security Issues

APPENDIX I: OBJECTIVES, SCOPE, AND METHODOLOGY

Our objectives were to answer the following research questions:

1. To what extent do the investment compositions of different target date funds (TDF) vary?
2. What is known about the performance of TDFs?
3. How do plan sponsors select and monitor TDFs that are chosen as the plan's default investment, and what steps do they take to communicate information on these funds to their plan participants?
4. What steps have the Department of Labor (DOL) and the Securities and Exchange Commission (SEC) taken to ensure that plan sponsors and participants appropriately select and use TDFs?

To answer the first question, we obtained and reviewed existing literature about TDFs and their investment approaches and interviewed a variety of retirement plan industry experts (see table 2 for a list of organizations we contacted). Second, we conducted case studies with eight TDF managers, which included in-depth semistructured interviews with representatives of the

TDF manager and reviewed available documents describing the nature of and reasons for TDF asset allocations. Through these discussions and reviews, we obtained detailed information on each provider's glide path philosophy, underlying funds and holdings, fee structure, and investment strategy and objectives. We also gained a fuller understanding of the investment philosophy, underlying assumptions, and concerns for different types of risks that underlie their approaches.

We selected eight TDF managers for cases studies to provide an understanding of the range of investment approaches taken by TDFs in the marketplace. These eight TDF managers we contacted reflect about 86 percent of the TDF market, by assets under management. Using Morningstar's *Target Date Series Research Paper: 2009 Industry Survey*, we selected TDF managers based on several criteria:

- **Size of assets under management:** We interviewed the top three TDF managers, whose funds account for over 70 percent of the TDF market, as well as other smaller fund managers, according to net asset information collected by Morningstar as of July 30, 2009.
- **Equity allocation at retirement:** We interviewed at least one manager with a high equity allocation (65 percent or more) in its 2010 fund and at least one manager with a low equity allocation (45 percent or less) in its 2010 fund.
- **Returns relative to size of equity allocation:** We interviewed fund managers whose 2010 funds performed either significantly better or worse in 2008 returns than other 2010 funds with relatively similar equity allocations. This factor was chosen because we wanted to understand what drove this difference in returns.
- **Active versus passive management:** We interviewed one fund manager that invested primarily in passively managed underlying funds and seven fund managers that invested primarily in actively managed underlying funds.
- **Length of glide path:** We interviewed at least one TDF manager who employs a "To" glide path (i.e., a glide path that ends at the retirement date) and at least one manager that employs a "Through" glide path (i.e., a glide path that continues to change after the retirement date). TDF glide paths were determined through TDF prospectuses, marketing materials, and Web sites and verified by fund managers.

To address the second question, on the performance of TDFs, we reviewed historical data and performed a literature review of studies completed that project the potential future long-term performance of TDFs. The historical data were obtained from Morningstar. We obtained return data from 2005 to 2009 for the largest 15 TDFs with at least 5 years of performance data. Some TDFs were not included in the sample because the funds had been in existence for less than 5 years. We interviewed Morningstar officials regarding the data's reliability and their processes for ensuring the reliability of their data, establishing that the data were both relevant and complete.

To determine the potential long-term performance of TDFs, we conducted a literature review and analyzed the results of selected studies. A literature review was conducted and documented with the help of the team librarian. Using a snowballing technique, the studies selected from the literature review were reviewed, and any other relevant articles mentioned in the studies initially selected through the literature review were obtained and then reviewed as well. Once this list of studies was compiled, the team contacted industry experts, knowledgeable stakeholders, and academics to review the list of studies compiled and identify any additional relevant studies. The new studies were then reviewed. We narrowed down our list of studies based on several screening criteria:

- Was the study based on original quantitative research using actual historical data, stochastic techniques, or other quantitative methods?
- Was the study free from bias and not conducted or commissioned by an organization that develops or markets TDFs or competing investment products or provides services and advice to plan sponsors about TDFs?
- Did the study pass GAO's data reliability standards for completeness, accuracy, and consistency of the data, ensuring that the study was free from bias?

Ultimately, nine studies were chosen based on the screening criteria and served as the basis of our findings on the potential future long-term performance of TDFs.

Table 2. Organizations Contacted during Review

Organizations contacted	Contact regarding objective:			
	1	2	3	4
TDF managers Eight firms that offer and manage TDFs	X	X		
Consultants and service providers • Aon Hewitt • Captrust Financial Advisors • Mercer • Summit Financial Group • Target Date Analytics • Towers Watson	X	X	X	
Government • Employee Benefits Security Administration (EBSA), DOL • U.S. Department of the Treasury • SEC	X	X	X	X
Plan sponsors Ten plan sponsors that use TDFs as their 401(k) plan default investment			X	
Other organizations • AARP • American Benefits Council • Academic Expert at Kennedy School of Government, Harvard University • Academic Expert at the University of California, Los Angeles • Academic Expert at the University of Chicago Booth School of Business • Academic Expert at University of Mississippi School of Law • Academic Expert of the Wharton School of the University of Pennsylvania • American Society of Pension Professionals and Actuaries (ASPPA) • Committee on Investment of Employee Benefit Assets (CIEBA) • Fiduciary Counselors • Investment Company Institute (ICI) • Morningstar • Profit Sharing/401k Council of America (PSCA) • Reish & Reicher	X	X	X	X

Source: GAO.

To answer the third question, we first reviewed relevant federal laws and regulations and relevant literature and spoke with federal officials and employee benefits attorneys to understand fiduciary requirements as they relate to qualified default investment alternatives (QDIA) and TDFs. Second, we interviewed key national organizations and pension industry experts to understand the concerns faced by plan sponsors and their participants regarding TDFs. This included representatives from organizations that represent plan sponsors, such as the Committee on Investment of Employee Benefit Assets, Profit Sharing/401(k) Council of America, and participants, such as AARP. In addition, we interviewed several plan consultants, such as Aon Hewitt, and several record keepers, such as Principal Financial Group, to understand how they work with plan sponsors to select and monitor TDFs. Third, we conducted 10 case studies with plan sponsors of all sizes, which included in-depth semistructured interviews and a review of relevant communication materials given to participants. Through these discussions and reviews, we obtained detailed information on their TDF selection process, ongoing due diligence monitoring activities, and communication provided to participants about TDFs. The results of our plan sponsor case studies were limited by the willingness of plan sponsors to speak with us.

We selected 10 plan sponsors for case studies using a two-step process. First, we used Form 5500 data from DOL to identify plan sponsors that have TDFs as an investment option in their 401(K) plans. We used the Form 5500 data to segment plan sponsors into three groups—small, medium, and large—based on the number of total active participants in their 401(k) plans. Small plans were defined as having 25 to 249 active participants, medium plans as 250 to 4,999 active participants, and large plans as 5,000 or more active participants. Second, we selected plan sponsors from each group to be interviewed as a case study based on three selection criteria: (1) industry of the plan sponsor, (2) level of industry wage earnings, and (3) TDF chosen as default investment. We determined the first criterion by using the North American Industry Classification System (NAICS) codes in the Form 5500 data. We chose plan sponsors across a variety of industries, including financial services, consumer products, professional services, educational services, and agriculture, among others. The second criterion was determined by using the U.S. Bureau of Labor Statistics' national monthly wage analysis data to determine if the plan sponsor is in either a high- or low-wage-earning industry. We chose plan sponsors in both high-wage and low-wage industries. We determined if plan sponsors met the third criterion by contacting the plan sponsor's staff in charge of human resources/benefits and through *Pensions &*

Investments data and other industry news articles, where available.[54] Ultimately, we chose to interview six large plan sponsors, two medium-sized plan sponsors, and two small plan sponsors.

To answer the fourth question, we reviewed relevant federal laws and regulations and interviewed agency officials as well as external experts to analyze recent actions taken by DOL and SEC regarding TDFs. First, we reviewed relevant federal laws and regulations that govern TDF disclosures and that govern the use of TDFs in defined contribution plans. Second, we interviewed DOL and SEC officials throughout our engagement and reviewed testimony and documents from the DOL-SEC joint hearing on TDFs in June and July 2009. Third, we reviewed recent actions taken by DOL and SEC, such as the DOL-SEC joint investor bulletin on TDF investing published in May 2010, and SEC's proposed regulation for the marketing and naming of TDFs, and EBSA's proposed regulation on target date disclosures. Finally, we reviewed comments submitted on recent proposed federal regulations and spoke with representatives of plan sponsors and plan participants, TDF managers, industry and academic experts, and national organizations that represent TDF managers.

APPENDIX II: STUDIES REVIEWED TO ASSESS RANGES OF FUTURE TDF PERFORMANCE

Basu, A. K., and M. E. Drew, "Portfolio Size Effect in Retirement Accounts: What Does It Imply for Lifecycle Asset Allocation Funds?" *Journal of Portfolio Management*, Spring (2009): 61-72.

Bodie, Z. and J. Treussard, "Making Investment Choices as Simple as Possible, but Not Simpler," *Financial Analysts Journal*, vol. 63, no. 3, (2007): 42-47.

Brady, P., "What Does the Market Crash Mean for the Ability of 401(k) Plans to Provide Retirement Income?" *National Tax Journal*, vol. LXII, no. 3 (2009): 455-476.

Bridges, B., R. Gesumaria, and M. Leonesio, "Assessing the Performance of Life-Cycle Portfolio Allocation Strategies for Retirement Saving: A Simulation Study," *Social Security Bulletin*, vol. 70, no. 1 (2010): 23-43.

Pang, G., and M. Warshawsky, "Asset Allocations and Risk-Return Tradeoffs of Target-Date Funds," *Journal of Pension Benefits*, (2010): 24-35.

Park, Y., "Plan Demographics, Participants' Saving Behavior, and Target-Date Fund Investments," *EBRI Issue Brief*, no. 329 (2009): 1-41.

Poterba, J., J. Rauh, S. Venti, and D. Wise, "Reducing Social Security PRA Risk at the Individual Level: Lifecycle Funds and No-Loss Strategies," *NBER Working Paper Series 06-07,* (2006): 1-43.

Shiller, R., "The Life-Cycle Personal Accounts Proposal for Social Security: An Evaluation," *NBER Working Paper Series 11300*, (2005): 1-34.

Spitzer, J., and S. Singh, "Shortfall Risk of Target-Date Funds During Retirement," *Financial Services Review*, vol. 17 (2008): 143-153.

End Notes

[1] Pub. L. No. 109-280 (2006) Section 902 of PPA added Code sections 401(k)(13), 401(m)(12) and 414(w). In 2009, the Internal Revenue Service promulgated final regulations addressing automatic enrollment. Automatic Contribution Arrangements, 74 Fed. Reg. 8,200 (February 24, 2009) (to be codified at 26 C.F.R. pts. 1 and 54).

[2] Morningstar is a provider of research that provides data on stocks, mutual funds, and similar vehicles.

[3] Congressional Research Service, *Pension Sponsorship and Participation: Summary of Recent Trends,* Washington, D.C.: Sept. 11, 2009.

[4]See GAO, *Retirement Savings: Automatic Enrollment Shows Promise for Some Workers, but Proposals to Broaden Retirement Savings for Other Workers Could Face Challenges*, GAO-10-31 (Washington, D.C.: Oct. 23, 2009).

[5] See § 624(a) of the PPA and 29 C.F.R. § 2550.404c-5.

[6] 29 CFR §2550.404c-5(e) In addition to these three QDIAs, a plan sponsor may also invest a participant's contributions in a capital preservation fund—a fund designed to preserve principal and provide a reasonable rate of return—for the first 120 days of participation. The final QDIA regulation was promulgated in 2007.

[7] See GAO-10-31.

[8] TDFs may also hold cash, and some also include investments in alternative assets, such as commodities.

[9] Among these laws are the Securities Act of 1933, 15 U.S.C s.77a et. seq. (Pub. L. No. 111-229); the Securities Exchange Act of 1934, 15 U.S.C. § 78a (Pub L. No. 111-257); the Investment Company Act of 1940, 15 U.S.C. s.80a-64 (Pub. L. No.111-257, as amended); and the Investment Advisers Act of 1940 (15 U.S.C. § 80b-1-§80b-21; Pub. L. No. 111-257).

[10] See 12 C.F.R § 9.18(a)(2). According to 2009 data compiled by Morningstar, about 79 percent of TDF assets were held in the form of mutual funds, and 16 percent were in the form of CITs. The balance was held in other forms.

[11] U.S. Senate Special Committee on Aging, *Target Date Retirement Funds: Lack of Clarity among Structures and Fees Raises Concerns*, Summary of Committee Research, prepared by the majority staff of the Special Committee on Aging, U.S. Senate, October 2009.

[12] Figure 3 includes only four examples for purposes of visual clarity. Of the eight TDFs included in our study, the illustration depicts TDFs with a relatively high and a relatively low allocation to equity at the retirement date, as well as two intermediate examples.

[13] According to officials at Morningstar, the large majority of TDFs used by retirement plans continue the glide path beyond retirement. Six of the eight TDFs included in our review do so.

[14] This TDF plan manager noted that a rule of thumb for spending in retirement is to withdraw only 4 to 5 percent of the initial savings amount to ensure savings are not depleted. Hence, a 5 percent withdrawal rate may be on the high side of what the analysis considered prudent.

[15] JP Morgan Asset Management, *Ready! Fire! Aim? 2009: How Some Target Date Fund Designs Continue to Miss the Mark on Providing Retirement Security for Those Who Need it Most*, December 2009.

[16] GAO-10-31.

[17] A fundamental approach to selecting equities considers all the factors that affect its cash flow, profits, the industry it operates in, and the economy in general. In contrast, a quantitative approach is a statistical approach and considers such factors as earnings momentum and price momentum.

[18] Investment-grade bonds are bonds with high credit ratings, meaning that the issuer is likely to meet its obligations, and can thus offer lower interest rates. High-yield bonds are bonds with a credit rating below investment grade. TIPS are securities whose principal is adjusted by changes in the Consumer Price Index. With inflation, the principal increases, and with deflation, the principal decreases. TIPS pay interest at a fixed rate, which is applied to the adjusted principal.

[19] According to investment theory, an efficient market is one in which the price of an asset reflects all information known about that asset, and therefore reflects its true value. As a result, there is little to no opportunity for investment managers to profit by consistently outperforming indexes of the broad market.

[20] According to this TDF manager, if the absolute return strategies are successful, they would outperform the general securities markets during periods of flat or negative market performance, underperform during periods of strong market performance, and typically produce less volatile returns than the general securities market.

[21] An option is the right to buy or sell a specific security at a specified price at or within a specified time. This may be done regardless of the current market price of the security. A futures contract is an obligation to make or take delivery of a specified quantity of an underlying asset at a particular future time at the price agreed on when the contract was made. A swap is a type of derivative in which two parties agree to exchange assets or cash flows over an agreed period. They can be based on equity indexes, bonds of different maturities, baskets of securities, individual securities, or interest rates.

[22] For purposes of this report, we define alternative assets as investments other than those intended to achieve exposure to equities, fixed income investments, or cash. Such investment can include real estate, commodities, and private equity.

[23] Josh Charlson, David Falkof, Michael Herbst, Laura Pavlenko, and John Rekenthaler, *Target Date Series Research Paper: 2010 Industry Survey*, Morningstar.

[24] Charlson and others, *Target Date Series Research Paper.*

[25] Charlson and others, *Target Date Series Research Paper.*

[26] For a listing of all nine studies we reviewed see appendix II.

[27] J. Poterba, J. Rauh, S. Venti, and D. Wise, "Reducing Social Security PRA Risk at the Individual Level – Lifecycle Funds and No-Loss Strategies," paper presented at the Eighth Annual Joint Conference of the Retirement Research Consortium, Washington, D.C. (2006). The authors calculate a wide range of outcomes based on education, investment strategy, and assumptions about historical asset return distributions. The authors model contributions to

retirement accounts over a participant's working life, until retirement at age 63, and combine these contributions with information on the simulated performance of different investment vehicles using actual lifetime earnings histories. They then carry out simulations for various earnings histories with simulated patterns of asset returns to make their conclusions. The authors structure their portfolios so that the percentage of stocks held in the portfolio is equal to the number 110 minus the age of the household head, with the remaining balance held in TIPS.

28 The study also reported that the outcomes for the lowest percentile of those with a high school diploma could possibly accumulate only about $83,000, while the outcomes for those in the 90th percentile could possibly accumulate $1,001,000—12 times the amount accumulated by the first percentile.

29 B. Bridges, R. Gesumaria, and M. Leonesio. "Assessing the Performance of Life-Cycle Portfolio Allocation Strategies for Retirement Saving: A Simulation Study." *Social Security Bulletin*, vol. 70, no. 1 (2010): 23-43.

30 In this study the baseline portfolio invests 85 percent of total value in equities through age 29, with the equity share declining linearly until it reaches 15 percent at age 60, where it remains thereafter. The remainder of the portfolio is invested in the bond fund. The bond fund consists of one-half long-term federal Treasury bonds and one-half 6-month private sector money market instruments.

31 The study conducted a series of stochastic simulations of 28 birth cohorts between 1915 and 1942, using historical investment returns for the years 1926 to 2008. The study was based on actual lifetime earnings histories. Real asset returns are derived by adjusting nominal values for inflation. Bridges and others, "Assessing the Performance of Life-Cycle Portfolio Allocation Strategies for Retirement Saving: A Simulation Study," 23-43.

32 Bridges and others, "Assessing the Performance of Life-Cycle Portfolio Allocation Strategies for Retirement Saving: A Simulation Study," 23-43.
The study, which used four TDFs that varied in terms of risk exposure and various participant ages, used historical return data in modeling the results. The aggressive TDF resulted in a real internal rate of return averaging 5.1 percent, with the outcomes ranging between -9.5 percent and 17.8 percent. By comparison, the conservative TDF had an average return of 3.9 percent. Returns for the conservative TDF ranged from -5.6 percent to 13.2 percent. The conservative TDF investment model started with 70 percent invested in equities through age 29 and then linearly declines to 10 percent at age 60.

33 A. K. Basu and M. E. Drew, "Portfolio Size Effect in Retirement Accounts: What Does It Imply for Lifecycle Asset Allocation Funds?" *The Journal of Portfolio Management*, Spring (2009): 61-72. This study used four hypothetical TDFs invested in equities, fixed income investments, and cash to perform the modeling.

34 John Spitzer and S. Singh. "Shortfall Risk of Target-Date Funds During Retirement," *Financial Services Review*, (2008): 143-153.

35 Bridges and others, "Assessing the Performance of Life-Cycle Portfolio Allocation Strategies for Retirement Saving: A Simulation Study," 23-43.

36 Some studies compared TDFs with other investment products and portfolios. However, for the purpose of this report we are focusing on balanced funds and all-bond funds.

37 Bridges and others, "Assessing the Performance of Life-Cycle Portfolio Allocation Strategies for Retirement Saving: A Simulation Study," 23-43.

38 According to the study, the 50/50 balanced fund average annual returns were 4.9 percent as compared with 4.2 for the conservative TDF, 4.6 for the moderate TDF, and 5.3 for the aggressive TDF respectively.

[39] P. Brady "What Does the Market Crash Mean for the Ability of 401(k) Plans to Provide Retirement Income?" *National Tax Journal*, vol. LXII, no. 3 (2009): 455-476.

[40] Bridges and others, "Assessing the Performance of Life-Cycle Portfolio Allocation Strategies for Retirement Saving: A Simulation Study." The study compared an all-bond fund composed of half long-term Treasury bonds and half 6-month private sector money market funds with a simulated TDF.

[41] ERISA fiduciaries are required to act solely in the interest of plan participants and their beneficiaries and select and monitor plan investments with the care, skill, prudence, and diligence under the circumstances then prevailing that a prudent man acting in like capacity and familiar with such matters would act. There are a number of steps plan sponsors should take when selecting and monitoring any type of investment in their 401(k)s, including reviewing fund fees and expenses to make sure they are reasonable, assessing and monitoring fund management, and reviewing performance periodically. 29 U.S.C.§ 1104.

[42] Plan participants can withdraw funds from a 401(k) account in advance of retirement through a number of means, such as a loan or a withdrawal due to financial hardship. See GAO, *401(k) Plans: Policy Changes Could Reduce the Long-Term Effects of Leakage on Workers' Retirement Savings*, GAO-09-715 (Washington D.C.: Aug. 28, 2009).

[43] Default Investment Alternatives Under Participant Directed Individual Account Plans; Final Rule, 72. Fed. Reg. 60,452, 60,461 (October 24, 2007) (codified at 29 C.F.R. pt. 2550). In the same preamble, DOL explained that with respect to balanced funds, another QDIA option, fiduciaries are required to take into account the demographics of the plan's participants in selecting a balanced fund as a QDIA. 72 Fed. Reg. 60,461, 60,462.

[44] According to a nationally recognized ERISA expert, such omissions may be considered a breach of fiduciary duty, in light of ERISA's requirement that plan sponsors prudently select and monitor plan investment options, and carefully consider the quality of competing providers and investment products, as appropriate.

[45] On October 22, 2010, DOL published a proposed rule to amend the definition of an ERISA fiduciary that would require any person, with certain exceptions, who gives advice or recommendations as to the selection of investment managers of plan assets to become an ERISA fiduciary. Definition of the Term "Fiduciary," 75 Fed. Reg. 65,263 (Oct. 22, 2010) (to be codified at 29 C.F.R. pt. 2550). A forthcoming GAO report will discuss the potential conflicts of interest of service providers offering advice to plan sponsors and plan participants in more detail.

[46] Retirement income replacement rates refer to the percentage of a participant's final salary that is matched by the participant's retirement payments, if the participant was to purchase an annuity with the balance of his or her retirement account at the retirement date.

[47] A record keeper is a service provider that provides record-keeping services such as plan administration, monitoring of plan and participant and beneficiary transactions (e.g., enrollment, payroll deductions and contributions, offering designated investment alternatives and other covered plan investments, loans, withdrawals, and distributions), and the maintenance of covered plan and participant and beneficiary accounts, records, and statements.

[48] Brightscope is an independent provider of 401(k) ratings and financial information to plan sponsors, advisers, and participants.

[49] DOL and SEC "Investor Bulletin: Target Date Retirement Funds," May 6, 2010.

[50] Investment Company Advertising: Target Date Retirement Fund Names and Marketing, 75 Fed. Reg. 35,920 (June 23, 2010) (to be codified at 17 C.F.R. pts. 230 and 270).

In: 401(k) Plans
Editor: Wesley Meyer

ISBN: 978-1-63484-727-8

Chapter 4

TARGET DATE RETIREMENT FUNDS - TIPS FOR ERISA PLAN FIDUCIARIES*

U.S. Department of Labor, Employee Benefits Security Administration

Target date retirement funds (also called target date funds or TDFs) have become an increasingly popular investment option in 401(k) plans and similar employee-directed retirement plans. The U.S. Department of Labor's Employee Benefits Security Administration (EBSA) prepared the following general guidance to assist plan fiduciaries in selecting and monitoring TDFs and other investment options in 401(k) and similar participant-directed individual account plans. Employers and other plan fiduciaries can learn more about their fiduciary responsibilities under the Employee Retirement Income Security Act of 1974 (ERISA) by visiting EBSA's website at www.dol.gov/ebsa/compliance_assistance.html.

TARGET DATE FUND BASICS

With the growth of 401(k) and other individual account retirement plans, many more participants are responsible for investing their retirement savings.

* This is an edited, reformatted and augmented version of a fact sheet issued by the U.S. Department of Labor, February 2013.

Target date retirement funds, or TDFs, can be attractive investment options for employees who do not want to actively manage their retirement savings. TDFs automatically rebalance to become more conservative as an employee gets closer to retirement. The "target date" refers to a target retirement date, and often is part of the name of the fund. For example, you might see TDFs with names like "Portfolio 2030," "Retirement Fund 2030," or "Target 2030" that are designed for individuals who intend to retire during or near the year 2030. Because of these features, many plan sponsors decide to use TDFs as their plan's qualified default investment alternative (QDIA) under Department of Labor regulations. A QDIA is a default investment option chosen by a plan fiduciary for participants who fail to make an election regarding investment of their account balances.[1]

TDFs offer a long-term investment strategy based on holding a mix of stocks, bonds and other investments (this mix is called an asset allocation) that automatically changes over time as the participant ages. A TDF's initial asset allocation, when the target date is a number of years away, usually consists mostly of stocks or equity investments, which often have greater potential for higher returns but also can be more volatile and carry greater investment risk. As the target retirement date approaches (and often continuing after the target date), the fund's asset allocation shifts to include a higher proportion of more conservative investments, like bonds and cash instruments, which generally are less volatile and carry less investment risk than stocks. The shift in the asset allocation over time is called the TDF's "glide path." It is important to know whether a target date fund's glide path uses a "to retirement" or a "through retirement" approach. A "to" approach reduces the TDF's equity exposure over time to its most conservative point at the target date. A "through" approach reduces equity exposure through the target date so it does not reach its most conservative point until years later.

Within this general framework, however, there are considerable differences among TDFs offered by different providers, even among TDFs with the same target date. For example, TDFs may have different investment strategies, glide paths, and investment-related fees. Because these differences can significantly affect the way a TDF performs, it is important that fiduciaries understand these differences when selecting a TDF as an investment option for their plan.

What to Remember When Choosing Target Date Funds

- *Establish a process for comparing and selecting TDFs.* In general, plan fiduciaries should engage in an objective process to obtain information that will enable them to evaluate the prudence of any investment option made available under the plan. For example, in selecting a TDF you should consider prospectus information, such as information about performance (investment returns) and investment fees and expenses. You should consider how well the TDF's characteristics align with eligible employees' ages and likely retirement dates. It also may be helpful for plan fiduciaries to discuss with their prospective TDF providers the possible significance of other characteristics of the participant population, such as participation in a traditional defined benefit pension plan offered by the employer, salary levels, turnover rates, contribution rates and withdrawal patterns.
- *Establish a process for the periodic review of selected TDFs.* Plan fiduciaries are required to periodically review the plan's investment options to ensure that they should continue to be offered. At a minimum, the review process should include examining whether there have been any significant changes in the information fiduciaries considered when the option was selected or last reviewed. For instance, if a TDF's investment strategy or management team changes significantly, or if the fund's manager is not effectively carrying out the fund's stated investment strategy, then it may be necessary to consider replacing the fund. Similarly, if your plan's objectives in offering a TDF change, you should consider replacing the fund.
- *Understand the fund's investments – the allocation in different asset classes (stocks, bonds, cash), individual investments, and how these will change over time.* Have you looked at the fund's prospectus or offering materials? Do you understand the principal strategies and risks of the fund, or of any underlying asset classes or investments that may be held by the TDF? Make sure you understand the fund's glide path, including when the fund will reach its most conservative asset allocation and whether that will occur at or after the target date. Some funds keep a sizeable investment in more volatile assets, like stocks, even as they pass their "target" retirement dates. Since these

funds continue to invest in stock, your employees' retirement savings may continue to have some investment risk after they retire. These funds are generally for employees who don't expect to withdraw all of their 401(k) account savings immediately upon retirement, but would rather make periodic withdrawals over the span of their retirement years. Other TDFs are concentrated in more conservative and less volatile investments at the target date, assuming that employees will want to cash out of the plan on the day they retire. If the employees don't understand the fund's glide path assumptions when they invest, they may be surprised later if it turns out not to be a good fit for them.

- *Review the fund's fees and investment expenses.* TDF costs can vary significantly, both in the amount and types of fees. Small differences in investment fees and costs can have a serious impact on reducing long term retirement savings.[2] Do you understand the fees and expenses, including any sales loads, for the TDF? If the TDF invests in other funds, did you consider the fees and expenses for both the TDF and the underlying funds? If the expense ratios of the individual component funds are substantially less than the overall TDF, you should ask what services and expenses make up the difference. Added expenses may be for asset allocation, rebalancing and access to special investments that can smooth returns in uncertain markets, and may be worth it, but it is important to ask.
- *Inquire about whether a custom or non-proprietary target date fund would be a better fit for your plan.* Some TDF vendors may offer a pre-packaged product which uses only the vendor's proprietary funds as the TDF component investments. Alternatively, a "custom" TDF may offer advantages to your plan participants by giving you the ability to incorporate the plan's existing core funds in the TDF. Non-proprietary TDFs could also offer advantages by including component funds that are managed by fund managers other than the TDF provider itself, thus diversifying participants' exposure to one investment provider. There are some costs and administrative tasks involved in creating a custom or nonproprietary TDF, and they may not be right for every plan, but you should ask your investment provider whether it offers them.
- *Develop effective employee communications.* Have you planned for the employees to receive appropriate information about TDFs in general, as a retirement investment option, and about individual TDFs available in the plan? Just as it is important for the plan

fiduciary to understand TDF basics when choosing a TDF investment option for the plan, employees who are responsible for investing their individual accounts need information too. Disclosures required by law also must be considered. The Department published a final rule that, starting for most plans in August 2012, requires that participants in 401(k)-type individual account retirement plans receive greater information about the fees and expenses associated with their plans, including specific fee and expense information about TDFs and other investment options available under their plans. The Department of Labor is also working on regulations to improve the disclosures that must be made to participants specifically about TDFs. For example, in addition to general information about TDFs, the proposed regulations call for disclosures to include an explanation that an investment in a TDF is not guaranteed and that participants can lose money in the fund, including at and after the target date. Check EBSA's website for updates on regulatory disclosure requirements.

- *Take advantage of available sources of information to evaluate the TDF and recommendations you received regarding the TDF selection.* While TDFs are relatively new investment options, there are an increasing number of commercially available sources for information and services to assist plan fiduciaries in their decision-making and review process.
- *Document the process.* Plan fiduciaries should document the selection and review process, including how they reached decisions about individual investment options.

RELATED INFORMATION

From the Department of Labor

- Investor Bulletin: Target Date Retirement Funds
- A Look at 401(k) Plan Fees
- Meeting Your Fiduciary Responsibilities
- Understanding Retirement Plan Fees and Expenses
- Understanding Your Retirement Plan Fees

- Selecting and Monitoring Pension Consultants – Tips for Plan Fiduciaries

From the SEC

- Beginners' Guide to Asset Allocation, Diversification, and Rebalancing
- Invest Wisely: An Introduction to Mutual Funds
- Mutual Fund Fees and Expenses

From the Financial Industry Regulatory Authority (FINRA)

- Fund Analyzer

End Notes

[1] More information on QDIAs is available in the Department's publication "Automatic Enrollment 401(k) Plans for Small Businesses" (available at http://www.dol.gov/ebsa/pdf/automaticenrollment401kplans.pdf).

[2] A difference of just one percentage point in fees (1.59 as compared with 0.59) over 35 years dramatically affects overall returns. If a worker with a 401(k) account balance of $25,000 averages a seven percent return, the worker will have $227,000 at retirement with the lower fee and $163,000 with the higher fee, assuming no further contributions. U.S. Department of Labor, Employee Benefits Security Administration, A Look At 401(k) Plan Fees, at http://www.dol.gov/ebsa/publications/401k_employee.html.

INDEX

D

E

I

L

M

S